Learn to
FRAME

Sheila Fairbrass

HarperCollins*Publishers*

Acknowledgements

I should like to thank the conservation and scientific colleagues who have patiently answered my questions; also Tony Stanlick of Framer's Equipment; David Nelson of Academy Framing, Burlington House; Daler-Rowney Limited; and all my friends who lent their pictures, and in one case their house, to be photographed for this book.

First published in 1990
by William Collins Sons & Co., Ltd
London · Glasgow · Sydney
Auckland · Toronto · Johannesburg

Reprinted by HarperCollins Publishers 1991

© Sheila Fairbrass, 1990

Art Editor: Caroline Hill
Layout by Joan Curtis
Photography by Jon Bouchier (pp. 1, 2, 4, 15, 21, 59, 63, 64)
and David Ridge (pp. 6, 9, 13, 16, 20, 24, 25, 29, 31, 36, 41, 45, 46, 55, 58)
Front cover photograph by Jon Bouchier
Illustrations by Tig Sutton
Filmset by Ace Filmsetting Ltd, Frome, Somerset
Colour reproduction by Bright Arts, Hong Kong

A CIP catalogue record for this book is available from the British Library

ISBN 0 00 412402 2

Printed and bound in Hong Kong

CONTENTS

INTRODUCTION

Before I start I'd like you to think about the last picture in a museum or art gallery that you really liked. Close your eyes for a moment and bring the image to mind. Now try to describe the frame. If you are like most people the picture will remain uppermost in your mind and you will have great difficulty in remembering the frame. This illustrates one of the most important characteristics of a frame – that it should complement and enhance the image but should never be so overwhelming that it completely dominates it visually.

Imagine, for instance, a subtle watercolour landscape, perhaps of mist rising over a lake. Using a heavy, dark moulding or even some ornate gilding to frame this sort of picture would completely detract from the image. On the other hand, a thin, pale oak frame would be totally lost around a vigorous, expressionist oil painting. It is all a matter of balance. In a very real way the frame contains the work of art, not just physically, but also visually. It defines the area of the picture and ensures that your eye is drawn to the work itself. Without a frame to present the painting it is very difficult mentally not to relate it to its surroundings, such as the lines of the window or the wallpaper.

A frame can also fulfil a second and, to my mind, equally valuable function. It can protect a work of art from damage. The two themes of presentation and protection will run throughout this book.

Conservation framing

My formal training is in conservation and I have specialized in paper conservation. Most of my time is taken up with restoring works of art such as prints, drawings and watercolours, which have been executed on paper. However, part of the conservation process is often concerned with framing the picture after its treatment. Frequently the damage caused to a picture is directly related to its frame and storage conditions. Most conservators agree that it is a waste of time working on an object only to find that it goes straight back into the conditions that caused the trouble in the first place. So all of us at some time or other show an interest in the subsequent storage and display of the restored object. This can range from designing a room to house a Viking longboat, writing the specifications for a display cabinet for a collection of glass, through to designing a picture frame for a Holbein drawing. In their basic forms all these examples are six-sided, sealed spaces containing an object of value.

In this book I shall cover all of the basic techniques you will need in order to mount, stretch and frame your own pictures, and on the way I shall also mention some of the other aspects you will need to consider if you decide it is important for you to protect and conserve your work. These include choosing the right material

4

which will cause as little damage or as few future problems as possible, and designing and making a frame which will provide some protection to the work of art. Both of these considerations come under the general heading of conservation framing.

On the whole it would be true to say that conservation framing will take you a little longer to do and will be slightly more expensive than the more conventional approach, which concentrates solely on the presentation part of the frame and spends very little time or energy considering the long-term effects that the materials used for framing might have on the work of art. You might also have to search a bit harder for some of

the materials I describe, but they are all available and quite often it is simply a matter of insisting on buying them and nothing else in their place. Don't be fobbed off with the excuse that conservation is only a fashionable whim and therefore not worth the bother in the long term. Since you are interested in learning to frame your own pictures you may as well do it properly. Those of you who are reading this book simply to get an overall view of the framing process might also find it useful to have some understanding of the basic ideas behind conservation framing so that the next time you speak to your framer you can discuss your needs with greater confidence. Most framers are very willing to try to do their best for your pictures.

In writing this book I have tried to tread the thin line between museum-standard framing, which often protects and displays priceless works of art and where the cost of the frame can be of less importance than the fact that it performs its job correctly, and commercial framing where the kind of frame that is made is often determined by how much the customer will pay. Many of the ideas behind conservation framing are common sense and, I hope, very obvious once they have been explained. When you have finished reading this book you should find that you have understood them and can apply the reasoning needed to make your own conservation-standard framing.

Design considerations

Before I go on I had better add a few words here about the design element of a frame. At various points in the book I shall no doubt break off to write a few words about the aesthetics of framing. Most of the other books I have read about framing try to offer advice on this subject and even proffer a few examples to be copied. In fact, some of them very quickly rush into illustrations of framed works of art and contain very little else. Personally, I find this very confusing and not much use. No-one is going to illustrate the perfect frame for my particular works of art. It is very much a matter of taste. I have my own ideas about design and they will no doubt become obvious as you read this book and look at the illustrations. But you might hate them! I could really no more tell you which moulding to put where than I could insist on the colour of the curtains you have in your living room. I want you to retain, or even engender, a fresh, individualistic approach to framing.

Some of the most successful frames have been made of materials which break all the rules. A case in point is the tiny oil painting of Battersea Power Station by Neil

Fig. 1 A series of Norman Ackroyd etchings balances the more elaborate style of the two mid twentieth-century oil paintings in the author's living room

5

Lloyd-Jones (**fig. 2**). The artist has chosen a wide, deep moulding to surround a painting which measures 150 × 230 mm (6 × 9 in). Because the moulding is stepped down it leads the eye into the picture; the thin gold fillet defines the picture area and separates the paint colours from the colour of the frame. The artist has given the wood a very thin coat of a water-based paint and then rubbed it down so that the grain and flaws in the wood show through. He has made no attempt at a 'perfect' frame. These slight inaccuracies mirror the handling of the oil paint itself.

If you decide to paint or stain the moulding yourself when you make your frames – and I hope you will attempt this at least once or twice and not rely solely on the finishes available in the shops – then be very careful with the colours you choose. In **fig. 2** the artist has used a neutral grey for the frame. There are several greys in the picture itself but none of them is exactly the same as the frame. If you deliberately use one of the colours in your picture you will immediately increase the overall amount of that colour which is presented to the eye.

This can distort the balance and harmony of your painting. On the other hand, some people find it quite pleasant to pick out one of the colours in this way. I am not saying it is wrong, just that you should be aware of what can happen.

When you are designing your frames, try not to be strange and wonderful in your approach simply for its own sake, however, since this often falls flat and looks contrived. As I mentioned earlier a frame should enhance and present your picture, not fight for your attention. Take the time to look closely at your paintings and choose their frames with care. If you are a painter or a collector, or you simply enjoy looking at beautiful things, follow your own instincts. Choose something you like and feel you could live with. If you are unsure about your own taste then start to be critical. Have a look at the frames of pictures in galleries. Start to notice how your friends have chosen their picture frames. Try to decide whether you feel they work. If you think that there is something wrong with them – and at this point I would advise a tactful silence if they are

Fig. 2 *Battersea Power Station* by Neil Lloyd-Jones

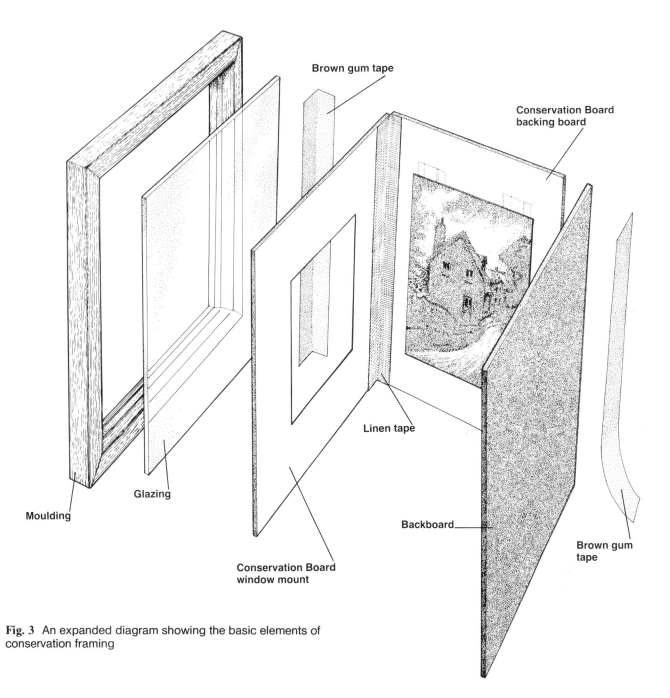

Brown gum tape

Conservation Board
backing board

Moulding

Glazing

Conservation Board
window mount

Linen tape

Backboard

Brown gum
tape

Fig. 3 An expanded diagram showing the basic elements of
conservation framing

your friend's choice – see if you can work out what it is
and how it could be put right.

The basic frame

So let's have a look at a basic frame and try to identify
the different components which make up this particular six-sided, sealed space.

Fig. 3 shows an expanded version of a frame for a
watercolour. I am starting with this because framing for
watercolours is what I know best, but please don't skip
this section simply because you always work in oils and
never touch watercolours. A basic frame is a basic
frame whatever it holds, and I want to cover some common ground here.

Four of the sides in the diagram are obviously the
moulding itself. We will examine these in more detail
and see how you can go about finding the most suitable
mouldings in the next chapter. The fifth side must be
the backboard, which leaves the sixth side as the glazing on the front. As long as they are strong and well
fitted together these six sides will form a long, narrow
box which will protect your picture. At this point, don't
worry about the extra bits in the diagram. These are
tapes and hinges and we will cover their use later on.
For the moment just look at the diagram and try to
imagine it squashed together so that the picture fits
behind the glass, the backboard fits behind the picture,
and the whole lot rests inside the frame. Now you can
see how the picture is protected on all six sides.

WHAT EQUIPMENT DO YOU NEED?

Fig. 4 illustrates all the equipment you might need to make frames. This chapter could easily start to sound like one of those cookery books which begin by listing the basic equipment you will require to start baking. No-one ever reads such a list! How many people inherit a kitchen and absolutely no equipment? In the same way, apart from some specialized machinery which I shall cover in greater detail along the way, I am going to suppose that you have, or can easily lay your hands on, most of the everyday tools in the photograph. Have another look and mentally tick off all the items that you know are around the house, or that you could borrow.

Tools   If you decide to make frames regularly you should think seriously about acquiring a set of good-quality tools, such as a hammer, bradawl, screwdrivers, hand-drill, pliers and clamps, which you will keep for your own use. There are various pieces of equipment that you can use for measuring, but it is important that once you start to make a frame using one kind of ruler or tape you keep to that one for the whole frame. They can all vary slightly and you will lose any accuracy if you chop and change mid-job. You will also find a good set square or T-square invaluable.

Moulding   You are going to need some moulding. I cover this subject in greater detail later (see page 11) but you should get into the habit of looking at the stock in framers' shops. Most of them have an oddments box with off-cuts and short lengths of moulding which they will sell cheaply. There may not be enough to make up a frame, but you could use them to build up your own library of samples and to practise cutting mitres. It is also a good idea to notice interesting architraves and mouldings in builders' merchants' yards in case you want to design your own moulding. Once again it will help if you can get some samples.

Equipment for cutting mitres   When you come to make your frame you will have to cut a mitre at each end of your moulding: that is, an angled cut at 45 degrees so that the pieces will fit together at right angles. There are

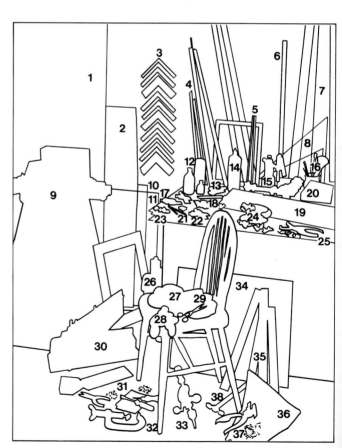

Fig. 4   Equipment for framing

 1 Hardboard
 2 Polycarbonate sheet
 3 Moulding samples
 4 Moulding (wood and metal)
 5 Balsa wood strips
 6 Rulers
 7 T-square
 8 Set squares
 9 Morso Cutter
10 Picture glass
11 Perspex
12 Fixatives and retouching varnish
13 Bamboo brushes
14 Wood-working adhesive
15 Underpinner
16 Brushes
17 Artists' paints
18 Craft knife
19 Mount cutter
20 Framer's gun
21 Pencils and eraser
22 Goldfinger
23 Mount boards
24 Hanging fittings and picture wire
25 Pliers and corner springs
26 Paints, varnishes and wood stains
27 Selection of tapes
28 Black velvet ribbon
29 Scissors
30 Mitre box with saw
31 Tools: saw, pliers, screwdriver and bradawl
32 G-clamp
33 Hand-drill
34 Stretched canvas
35 Stretcher pieces
36 Unprimed canvas
37 Canvas pliers and tacks
38 Hammer

several machines which will help you cut a piece of wood in this way. If you are serious about making frames then you should consider buying a proper framer's mitre box, such as the one illustrated in **fig. 5**. This will demand a similar outlay to that of buying, say, an electric drill. A cheaper, though far less satisfactory alternative is to buy a simple mitre block from a tool supplier. This is a wooden box with slots cut in it to guide the saw. Depending on your skill with a saw it will give you a cut of approximately 45 degrees. Unfortunately, however, the success or failure of your finished frame will depend almost entirely on the accuracy of the mitres. If your corners do not meet correctly it is impossible to cover up the fact. You can get away with using only the simple mitre block if you really have no alternative, but it is unlikely you will end up with a professional-looking frame, and the frustrations of trying to cope with such an inaccurate piece of equipment could well spoil the enjoyment of making your own frames. In the long term it will be well worth your while to start off with the proper tools. Beg, borrow or buy a mitre box. Better still, ask for one for your next birthday.

Whether you are cutting by hand or with the mitre box you will need a good saw. The mitre box in **fig. 5** and the one in **fig. 4** both come with their own integral saw. In any case you should check the blade and change it if necessary. The thicker and coarser the blade you use, the rougher will be the cut that you make. Remember that you are aiming for precision so ignore the wood saws and buy one with a blade for cutting metal. A hacksaw blade will do so long as it has fine teeth.

If you belong to an art club or society it might be worth your while looking into the possibility of collectively buying a Morso Cutter. This is really professional. It consists of a foot-operated guillotine which cuts the moulding cleanly at precise angles every time. A word of warning, however: because it is a professional's machine it needs professional care. It is also quite dangerous in that the blades are deadly sharp a[nd] even a moment's inattention can result in a nasty c[ut]. If your art club does decide to invest in one of the[se] cutters then be sure to take the retailer's advice abo[ut] setting it up correctly and how to use it safely.

Underpinner The other main piece of equipment th[at] you might not recognize in **fig. 4** is the underpinn[er]. This is used to attach the separate pieces of mouldi[ng] together to make the frame. It is not a vitally necessa[ry] tool and you can make your frames very easily witho[ut] it. It does, however, speed up the process considerab[ly] and you might be interested in buying one if you a[re] going to be making frames over a long period of time. [I] describe its use more fully in the chapter on making t[he] frame (see page 19).

Glazing The subject of different glazing materials [is] covered in more detail in the chapter on glazing (s[ee] page 22). As well as glass, Perspex or Plexiglass can [be] used. Notice that the Perspex in the illustration is [at] least the same thickness as the glass; in fact, it is pro[b]ably a bit thicker. Thin sheets of Perspex are a waste [of] your money since they afford no real protection to t[he] work of art. You will need to cut through the Persp[ex] with a saw. If you can cut it with a knife then it is pro[b]ably too thin to be used. To cut the glass, of course, yo[u] will need a glass cutter.

Backboards I have included hardboard (Masoni[te]) and polycarbonate sheeting as examples of suitab[le] backboard materials. The polycarbonate she[et] illustrated happens to be black, but you can buy exact[ly] the same material in a transparent sheet at builde[rs'] merchants and large do-it-yourself chain stores, whe[re] it is sold as a roofing material. It can be cut quite easi[ly] with a sharp knife. The piece of equipment that loo[ks] like a staple gun is, in fact, a framer's gun. This fires fl[at] metal pieces into the back of the moulding to hold t[he] backboard in place.

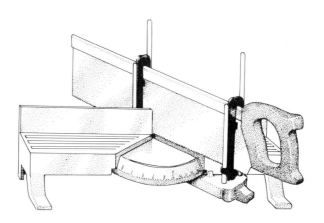

Fig. 5 A mitre box with integral saw

Mount boards and mount cutters The examples of coloured mount board are from the Daler Studland range of boards, which are readily available in a wide range of colours. Make sure that the colours you choose are labelled Conservation Quality since some of the boards in this range are ordinary mounting boards (that is, they are not acid-free) and they cannot be used in conservation framing. The cream and white boards are from the Daler Studland Museum range and are the kind I use in my work as a conservator. This board is also available in silver grey. I like them because one side of the board has a smooth surface and the other side a textured one; in this way you get a choice of surfaces on the same board. I tend to use the textured side most often since I like the slightly more opulent feel to it. It also seems to hide any mistakes I might make when cutting the bevelled aperture. Slight overcuts, which are glaringly obvious in a smooth-surfaced board, merge into the textured side of this Museum board. Even though I do not use Conservation Board for remounting pictures when I have treated them I usually have a few packets of it in my studio. I use it to make folders for storing valuable works of art in my plan chests.

If you intend to cut a number of mounts over a long period of time you will need a mount cutter. The one illustrated in **fig. 4** is the Logan Compact, but examples of different kinds of mount cutters are also included in the chapter on framing watercolours (see **fig. 34**).

Tapes You will also require a selection of different kinds of adhesive tapes. The brown paper tape illustrated is the kind you will find at a stationer's. It has an adhesive that needs to be wet in some way to make it stick. This is a general, all-purpose tape that is used to seal various parts of the frame. You should buy it in at least two widths – one broad, one narrow – or be prepared to trim it down to size. The white tapes are conservation-quality tapes and are used near, or next to, the work of art. One of them is called linen tape, although in fact it has a cotton backing. It is very strong and is used to hinge two pieces of mount board together to make a window mount. Some window mounts, especially those for modern works of art, can be comprised of two complete sheets of Museum Board, which makes them quite heavy. In these cases the hinging tape needs to be very sturdy to take the weight, so linen tape is ideal. The other tape illustrated is an acid-free paper tape, called framer's tape, which can be used to hinge works of art which are on robust paper such as cartridge paper. Both of these white tapes have an adhesive which you must wet to activate.

What appears to be black tape is in fact black velvet ribbon. You will need this if you are framing an oil or acrylic painting on a stretcher in a frame with no glazing. If you are reading through this book for the first time you could let your imagination run on at this point and try speculating on what possible use you might have for black velvet ribbon in framing (answer on p. 54)! Masking tape is required only if you want to make your own moulding. The transparent tape is 3M Magic Tape, which you might need if you decide to glaze your frame with Perspex. That is the only use for it in framing.

Canvas This can be bought in its raw state or ready-primed. The primer, which is the white coating on the canvas, can be either oil- or acrylic-based. If you intend to stretch your own primed canvas you will need some canvas pliers. These grip the canvas in their toothed ends so that you can pull it firmly over the stretcher piece. You might need some raw canvas as a backing if you are framing textiles or needlework. This is explained more fully in the chapter on framing a needlework (see page 58).

Hanging fittings When you have finished making your frame, and used it to display a painting, you will have to decide which method to use to hang it on the wall. There are various ways of doing this and to a certain extent the kind of frame you have made will dictate the manner in which it is hung. A small selection are shown in **fig. 4** but specific hanging fittings are described in more detail on page 40.

Other equipment The pair of pliers and metal springs are one way of holding the corners of the frame steady while waiting for the adhesive in the joints to dry. As I explain later there are many different ways of doing this and most framers' suppliers have their own preferred equipment, designed especially for this job. If you cannot find the particular items I have shown then have a look at what else is on offer. Most of the solutions differ more in price than effectiveness.

I have included in **fig. 4** a motley collection of paint tins, varnishes and wood stains. You will need to make your own collection if you are going to design your own frames. If you are an artist I shall not have to remind you how this type of equipment seems somehow to collect itself together until one day it takes over all of the available room! You will also need some artists' paints, such as the watercolour, gouache and oil paints in the Daler-Rowney ranges. In addition, Goldfinger, an all-purpose rub-on metallic paste for retouching the pin holes in the corners of your frame, will be useful.

Choosing a moulding

Mouldings are usually made of wood and they form the attractive border around the picture. As we go through this book I shall be referring to the different parts of a piece of moulding, which can be confusing at first, so

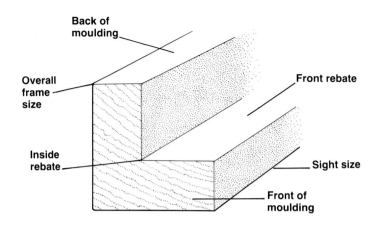

Fig. 6 Cross section of a simple moulding

take a look at **fig. 6**, which identifies them. If you were to saw through the simplest moulding it would have an L-shaped section. The glass, the picture and the backboard rest against the foot of the L. The front of the L is the front of the frame, the part that you see surrounding the picture. The sight size of a frame is measured from the front of the L. Sight size means the size of the picture area that you can see when you look at the frame from the front. The inside rebate measurement is taken from the inside corner of the L, and the overall frame size is measured along the back of the L. This measurement is taken by turning the frame over and measuring the back.

Before you go to the shop to choose your moulding, have a good look at the picture you are going to frame and perhaps make some notes on the kind of framing you would like. If you intend to frame several works, sort them into categories of pictures which might need similar frames. If possible, take one or two of them with you to the framing shop. If you are going to attempt conservation framing you should take a small ruler or tape measure along as well.

Walking into a framing shop is like going into Aladdin's cave. You seem to be surrounded by mouldings of every shape and colour imaginable. Take a deep breath and look around carefully. The designs will fall into well-defined categories. Some of the wood will be plain and uncoloured, or perhaps simply varnished. Other mouldings will be gilded. The latter always seem to be the first to catch the eye. They are also usually the most expensive. Another section might have mouldings which are plain in shape but lacquered with all the colours of the rainbow. Often the manufacturer will have taken a single wooden design, called a section, and treated it in different ways by gilding or painting or even printing on it, so that sometimes it is difficult at first to realize that it is the same moulding. Start by looking at the shape of the side, or cross section, of the

mouldings and when you have sorted that out, pick the colour or finish. You will generally find that the moulding you have chosen is available in many different colours or textures.

The mouldings illustrated in **fig. 7** are by no means an exhaustive selection. I have included some plain wood, some textured and some gilded mouldings. More importantly, they are all different cross sections. The gilded frames are not real gold or silver leaf, by the way. This type of gilding is a specialized craft, usually done to order, which is the reason they are quite expensive. The mouldings in the photograph are all deep enough to make a secure frame – an important point, which I explain below – except for the small gold and silver fillets at the bottom, which are made to slip inside the front of the frame between the moulding and the glass. This tiny metallic edging can turn even the plainest of wooden mouldings into something special. If you look back to the Neil Lloyd-Jones picture in **fig. 2** you will see an example of how to use this type of moulding to advantage.

You might have noticed that I have not included any examples of aluminium or metal frames in this selection. These present special difficulties in cutting and assembling and I shall deal more fully with these problems later (see page 20). If you want to use metal frames – and certainly their clean, clinical lines can set off some modern prints very well – then you will find a range of them, ready-cut to standard sizes, in most art shops. Daler-Rowney, for example, supply several different framing systems of this kind.

If you are trying conservation framing, to frame your picture properly and safely you will need a moulding at least 10 mm (⅜ in) deep for a work on paper and 28 mm (1⅛ in) deep if the picture has been stretched round a wooden stretcher (check **fig. 3** again).

I will warn you now that this is going to limit your choice severely. For many years manufacturers of

12

Fig. 7 A selection of mouldings suitable for conservation framing

framing materials have concentrated their efforts on designing the front of the moulding. The amount of wood for the depth of the moulding, which is equally important for a good frame, has often been scrimped to cut down costs. As you probably know, it costs more to buy a piece of battening which is 20×20 mm (¾ × ¾ in) in cross section than one that is 10×20 mm (⅜ × ¾ in). So, if the moulding looked the same on the front but was only half as deep, and the customer didn't seem to notice, it made sense to save money in this way. Unfortunately, as you will realize as you read through this book, it is impossible to make a safe, sturdy frame with thin moulding. Luckily, this cost-cutting approach is starting to change and some of the more forward-looking manufacturers are now adding generously cut mouldings to their ranges. However, be prepared to find that the majority of mouldings, although very pretty, are still of little use to you. If you use an inadequate moulding, even though you might fulfil the presentation requirement of the frame, as far as protection goes you might just as well paint the frame onto the canvas, or draw it round your watercolour.

So, armed with this knowledge and your ruler, go round the shop, carefully measuring the depth of the mouldings, and make your own small collection of suitable pieces. Then take a look at the prices of the ones you have chosen and make a second, even smaller selection of those within your price range. Now see if any of these will suit your picture. I selected the mouldings in **fig. 7** in exactly this way.

Mouldings are generally displayed as corner pieces, like the ones in **fig. 7**. If you have taken any pictures with you, slip one into the corner of a moulding. You will need a bit of imagination to visualize the other two sides of the frame, but even this small amount of moulding will usually give you some indication of whether it will suit your painting. Check on the colour or tone first. Does it enhance the tonal quality of your picture or does it deaden the composition? As I mentioned above, does it bring out one colour to the detriment of all the others and spoil the balance of the work? Does it clash horribly with the painting? Do you want to clash horribly with the painting? Is the moulding itself so finicky that it distracts the eye? Or have you found just the right thing? Take your time and decide.

If you find nothing that fulfils all the criteria of correct depth, reasonable price and suitability for your picture, then go and shop somewhere else. You are going to have to live with these frames for the next few years so make sure you start off with something you really like.

Making your own moulding

If you have not found a suitable moulding in your framing shop you should think about constructing your own. Most builders' merchants sell a wide range of architectural mouldings and wooden edgings. These look the same as picture mouldings but do not have the rebate on the back.

Fig. 8 shows how you can make a deep rebate by attaching a wooden batten to the back of a flat wooden section. Stick the batten in place with a good wood-working adhesive. You will need to use G-clamps to hold the moulding firmly between two long pieces of wood while it is drying. When it is totally fixed, remove the clamps and pieces of wood, then reinforce the join with veneer pins tapped in from the back every 150 mm (6 in) or so.

An alternative to using G-clamps after you have stuck the wooden section and batten together is to bind them firmly with masking tape. This method can only be used on plain wood since the tape will probably damage any finish or paint when you remove it. Wait until you have constructed the frame before you paint or stain the moulding.

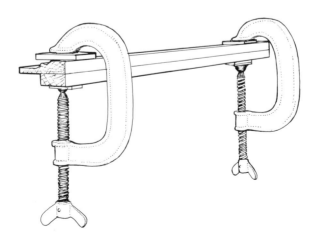

Fig. 8 Attaching a wooden batten to the back of a flat wooden section

9 When trying out a new style of framing, leave the picture in a prominent place to see if you can live with it

MAKING THE FRAME

Now that you have the equipment and materials you need you can start to construct a basic frame and then use this to frame a watercolour. There are two difficult steps in the process. The first is cutting the wood for the mouldings at an angle of exactly 45 degrees so that the pieces fit together at right angles to make a rectangular frame; the second is cutting the bevelled opening in a piece of card so that you can display the watercolour in the traditional way. Don't worry. As for most things in life, machines have been invented to help you through these difficult tasks.

Determining the frame size

First of all you have to decide how big you want your frame to be. This problem really only applies to works of art on paper, which will need a window mount. As I shall explain later, a painting on a stretcher is me[asur]ed in a different way and you do not have to dec[ide] on the side of the border. There are rules for establi[sh]ing the size of a window mount. They involve decid[ing] on the proportions of the visible painting and th[en] relating the width of the borders to these. Personall[y] have never understood them and my way is based [on] more on experience and rule of thumb.

Probably the easiest way to start is to work it all [out] by sight. Lay a large, clean piece of card or paper on [the] table or floor. If you are using a coloured mount boa[rd] lay this on top. Put your painting in the middle a[nd] arrange your moulding, or pieces of wood of a simi[lar] thickness, in a rectangle around it, allowing for [the] margins of the mount. Move the moulding about un[til]

Fig. 10 Working out the size of the frame

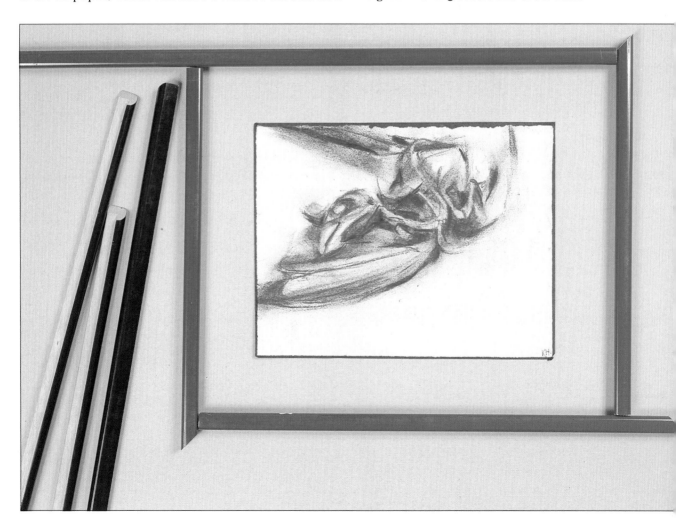

ou get the balance you want (**fig. 10**). Allow at least 0 mm (2 in) around a small watercolour and be more enerous with larger ones. Once again it all depends n taste. Some pictures look better with small margins nd narrow mouldings, while others just look cramped nd mean. When you are satisfied with the position of our moulding, measure the outside edges of the rame' – first the height, then the width. Round these measurements up or down to the nearest 12 mm (½ in) o determine your overall frame measurements. You ill need these when you come to cut your moulding.

utting the moulding

ou should always cut the longest sides of your frame rst. If you start by cutting one of the shortest edges and

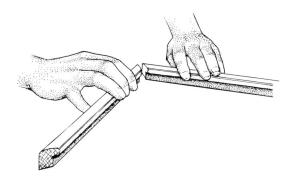

ig. 11 When you have made the first cut, check carefully hat the back edge of the moulding is longer than the ront edge

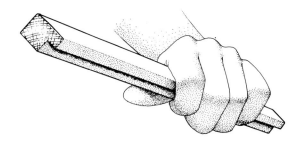

ig. 12 After cutting the second piece, lay the two pieces of houlding on the bench or work table and make sure that they ill fit together to form a right angle

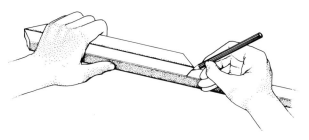

ig. 13 Lay the moulding back to back and mark off the econd piece accurately, using the first piece as a guide

something goes wrong you will end up with a useless piece of wood. If you make a mistake with a long piece, however, you can always cut a short side out of it.

The retailer might have cut you some moulding, or you might have bought standard lengths. Either way the ends will be cut square and you will need to mitre them so that they will fit together at right angles to each other. Put the end of the wood in your mitre box and cut your first mitre near the end of the moulding. You need to angle the saw so that the back edge of the moulding is longer than the front. Take the wood out of the mitre box and check that this is so (**fig. 11**).

Now remember that you are using the measurement of the longest edge first. Starting from the mitred edge, use a pencil to mark the longest of your frame measurements on the outside edge of the moulding. This is the side of the moulding which will be the outside edge of your finished frame. Put the moulding back in the mitre box and line up the saw with your pencil mark. This time you want the cut to slope the other way so that the two mitred edges point towards each other. They should not lie parallel. After you have made the second cut, check again that the two mitres slope towards each other and that the back edge of the moulding is longer than the front (**fig. 12**).

To cut the second long side, lay the first cut piece back to back against the rest of the moulding. Line up the bottom edges exactly by resting them gently on the bench or work table and mark the height of the first piece on the back of the second (**fig. 13**). Use this mark to cut the other long side. Remember before you cut this piece that, just like the first piece, the two mitres at either end of the wood must point towards each other and the back edge must be longer than the front. When you have done this you will have the two opposite sides to your frame and they should be exactly the same size. Make sure that this is so and be really honest with yourself. If the sides are not precisely the same length then the corners will not fit together accurately when you come to make up the frame.

Starting again from the mitred edge on the remainder of the moulding, mark the measurement of the shorter side along the back edge. Cut the short sides of your frame in exactly the same way as the long ones, checking each step as you go along. When you have cut all four pieces to size, lay them out on the bench or work table and push them together at the corners so they form a rectangle.

Congratulations! You've cut your first frame.

Gluing and pinning

The four pieces of moulding are joined by gluing and pinning. This might seem somewhat excessive. Why not save time and use one or the other? Well, the gluing keeps the moulding in place and stops it moving out

17

of line. The pins are necessary and take the weight of the glass, artwork and backboard when the picture is hanging on the wall.

Before putting the moulding together you might need to sand the cut edges very slightly to give a smooth surface. You should have a nice clean cut so there is no need to be heavy-handed. Tape a piece of fine sand-paper to the bench or work table and gently rub the cut surface across it. Then paint a wood-working adhesive on the mitred edges of the moulding and match them together to form the frame (**fig. 14**). Be very careful not to get any adhesive on the front of the moulding. If you do you can wipe it away but there will almost certainly be a slight residue left on the wood and this will show up as a different coloured patch if you try to stain the wood later on.

Make sure that the mitres and all of the decoration on the front of the moulding line up exactly before you leave your frame to dry. To make a strong bond you will need to clamp the joined pieces firmly together in some way while they dry. There are several types of corner clamp available, consisting of either plastic or metal right angles which fit on the corners and a strap that tightens round the frame. Ask in framing shops and see which kind they recommend. It is simply a matter of finding a system that suits you. A really good method is to use corner springs (**fig. 15**). These are strong metal grips which are opened out and slipped on to either side of the corner of the frame. Once in place they close up tightly and hold the moulding while it dries. They can be left in place overnight and removed when the adhesive is totally dry. Corner springs are very effective and simple to use and there is no chance of the mould-ing moving. Their only slight disadvantage is that they can leave small dents in the wood, but these can be filled and retouched when you fill the pin holes.

The panel pins are inserted into the corners of the frame across the mitred joint. Turn the frame over and look at the back. Hold one of the pins across the joint and check if it is the right size. It will need to reach from the outside edge of the moulding to the other side of the

mitred joint. It is certainly easier if you hold the frame steady in a carpenter's vice while putting in the pins.

First decide which way up the frame is going to hang and then tap one or, even better, two pins into the top and bottom corners on the sides. **Fig. 16** shows two

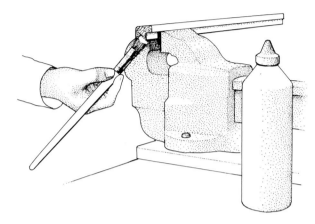

Fig. 14 Gluing the mitred edge

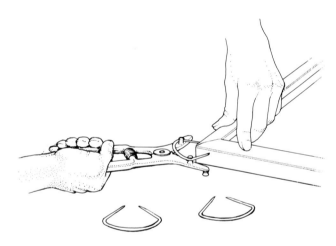

Fig. 15 Using corner springs to hold the moulding in place while the adhesive dries

Fig. 16 (*below*) Alternative methods of pinning the moulding

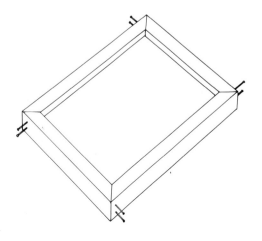
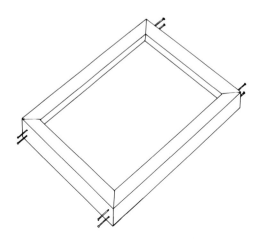

ternative ways of positioning the pins. Tap the pins raight into the wood so that they go across the mitre nd into both pieces of moulding (**fig. 17**). Unless you e a wizard with a small hammer you might find it sier to drill holes in the moulding first before you tap the pins. For perfect results, countersink the heads of e pins into the wood with a nail punch, then fill the

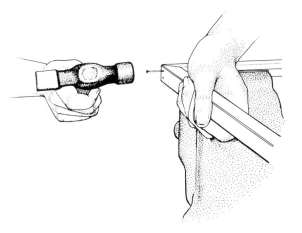

g. 17 Pinning the corners

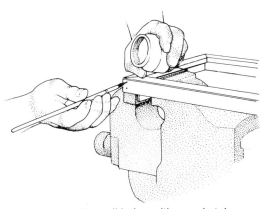

ig. 18 Retouching the nail holes with wood stain, gouache Goldfinger

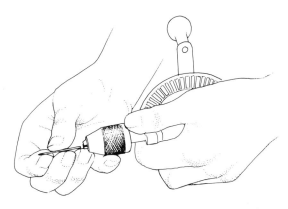

g. 19 Using a panel pin as a drill bit to make the holes efore pinning

holes level with the surface using wood filler. When this has dried, retouch the light patches with wood stain or gouache if the moulding is coloured, or Daler-Rowney's Goldfinger if you are making a gilded frame. With practise you should be able to tone in the patches and hide the nail holes (**fig. 18**).

The absolute perfectionists among you could try taking one of the panel pins, clipping off the head, and using the pin as the bit in a hand drill to make the holes (**fig. 19**). This should give you a hole of exactly the same size as the panel pins which you are using to secure the corners.

Decorating your own frames

Those of you who made your own moulding at the beginning should varnish, stain or paint your frame now. Even if you want a plain wooden frame I would still advise you to give the moulding a coat of varnish. A wooden surface picks up dirt and fingerprints surprisingly easily and these marks are quite difficult to remove. Give the frame two or three thin coats of clear wood varnish, allowing each coat to dry before applying the next.

There are various brands of wood stain on the market. They colour the wood so that the grain is still visible. If you want the wood grain completely hidden, however, you should paint the frame. Use a household emulsion and apply two or three thin coats rather than one thick, uneven one. There is of course no limit to the effects you can achieve with paint. For example, have a look at the spray paints, especially the metallic car paints, that are available. Try flecking or rag rolling your frames. As you gain confidence in your abilities and more experience in designing your own frames you will probably find that there is great satisfaction in producing exactly the right finish to suit your pictures.

Underpinning

Underpinning is an alternative to using panel pins. Almost all commercial framers use a piece of equipment called an underpinner rather than tap panel pins into the sides of the frames. Underpinners fire strong, barbed staples into the back of the moulding across the corners. These machines range from the hugely expensive ones where the staples are fired by compressed air and which do everything except make you a cup of tea afterwards, to simple hand-operated versions which are easy to use. Once again, if you are thinking of taking up framing as a permanent hobby or you belong to an art club which runs to more costly equipment, then you should look into the possibility of buying a simple underpinner.

An underpinner is used once you have glued your moulding together and it is completely dry. Place one

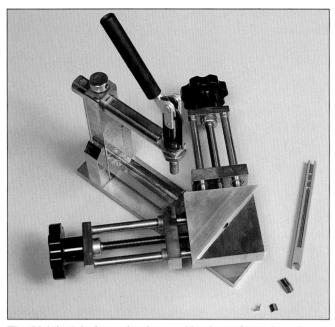

Fig. 20 (*above*) An underpinner with a box of metal staples

Fig. 21 (*right*) The contemporary gold metal frames of the pastels compliment the Victorian style of this bathroom

corner of your frame, face up, between the clamps. The V-shaped pieces of metal are the staples which are pushed into the back of the moulding across the mitred joints. Each corner is treated in turn. Using an underpinner is certainly a lot faster than drilling and pinning, and it makes a secure joint. You will have to offset these advantages against the cost of the initial outlay on the equipment and also the fact that, as a process, it uses a certain amount of force and the result is therefore very mechanical. You have more fine control with the longer, more traditional method using panel pins.

As I mentioned in the section on choosing your moulding, frames made totally from aluminium or metal section need specialist equipment and expertise to cut them and fit them together. There is a range of mouldings made with a wooden core and a thin metal sheet wrapped around it. This can be mitred and made up like an ordinary wooden moulding yet the finished article looks like a metal frame. Unfortunately, you will definitely need an underpinner to join the moulding securely. In most cases the inner wooden section has been pared down and is far too thin to hold together simply with glue. Because of the metalled sides you cannot pin through the corners, so underpinning is essential. This also applies to many of the mouldings with lacquered finishes that you will find in the shops. They have a mirror-like surface to them which would be totally spoiled by drilling and pinning through the corners. I am afraid, therefore, that in this case traditional methods can only be used for traditional frames.

GLAZING THE FRAME

Now you have the moulding fixed you can begin to think about the glazing. This is the sixth side of our box. Obviously in order to give any kind of protection it has to be fairly rigid. There are various makes of inexpensive plastic sheeting on the market which are transparent enough to be used as glazing but which are far too flexible to be considered. You should be able to stand the glazing upright on the floor, steadying it only with your hand on the top edge. If it bows alarmingly or, worse still, will not remain upright, then it is not rigid enough to use as glazing in your frame. In addition to this, most of the cheaper plastic sheets will slowly turn yellow in the light. The simplest, cheapest, most readily available suitable material for glazing frames is picture glass, which is 2 mm (1/16 in) thick.

Later on I shall show examples of oil paintings where it is possible to omit the glazing, but for any work of art on paper, or indeed any potentially fragile object such as needlework, it is important that the frame is glazed. Even in the cleanest house objects slowly get covered with a layer of dust. This includes not only horizontal surfaces but vertical ones as well, so leaving a watercolour unglazed means that it will get dirty.

To determine the size of your piece of glass, measure the height and width of the inside rebate of your frame and deduct 2 mm (1/16 in) from each figure. This will ensure that the glass will fall neatly into the frame. Don't be tempted to make the measurement a bit on the small side 'just in case'. Glass which is too small for the frame will inevitably slip to the bottom, leaving a gap at the top which will let in the dirt.

Cutting the glass

I would advise you always to buy your glass ready cut to size from the glass merchant. He will cut glass quickly, cheaply, and with right angles every time. I have watched a professional glass cutter at work. He made it look terribly easy. So much so, in fact, that when I need glass I go down to the shop and ask the glass merchant to cut it for me. It costs very little.

However, for those of you who like to do the complete job yourselves the following method is one of the simplest ways to cut glass. You will need a glass cutter. Some professionals swear by the oil-lubricated ones but the simple wheel or diamond cutters in most hardware stores are perfectly satisfactory (**fig. 22**).

Clean the glass and place it on a clean, flat surface. Glaziers cover their working surface with a soft,

non-woven fabric such as felt. Should you use felt or blanket, please be sure not to use it for anything else afterwards: it might have tiny specks of broken glass in it. Mark off your first measurement using a stiff metal or wooden rule and a T-square (**fig. 23**). Next, line up a stout metal straightedge along the T-square. You must use a straightedge that is larger than the piece of glass. You cannot score half the glass then move the straightedge down and score the other half. If you were to do so, when you came to snap the glass it would splinter where the two cuts met. Hold your glass cutter upright like a pencil (**fig. 24**) and score the glass gently but firmly. Listen to the noise it makes. It should hiss down the glass. If the noise changes or it starts to grate then you have changed the angle of the cutter and are scoring at a different depth. The idea is to break the tension on the top surface of the glass only. When you come to bend the glass and break it you will hopefully open up this crack, which will then run straight down through the glass and snap cleanly.

It might seem more logical to grasp the cutter in your fist and gouge out as deep a line as you can in the belief that if you cut as much as possible with the cutter then there is less to snap apart afterwards. However, unless you can score a line which is exactly the same depth from one end to the other – impossible to do manually – you will not be able to control the direction of the break going through the glass and it is more likely to shatter unevenly when you come to snap it.

To complete the cut, place your straightedge under the glass and line it up with the scored line. Put your

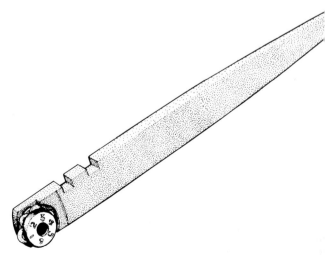

Fig. 22 A simple, easily available glass cutter

ands on either side of the scored line and press down ently (**fig. 25**). You should get a clean break. Resist the emptation to lean forwards and watch while the glass reaks. Keep your head up and your face at a safe istance away.

Now I know the first thing you are going to do, having just read the above, is find some old glass to practise n. By all means practise, but do it on small pieces of ew glass. You will find it much easier to manage.

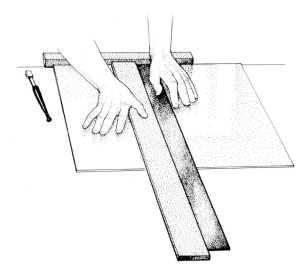

Fig. 23 Using a T-square and metal straightedge to align the cutting edge at right angles to the edge of the glass

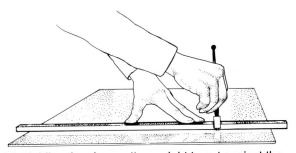

Fig. 24 Holding the glass cutter upright to cut against the metal straightedge

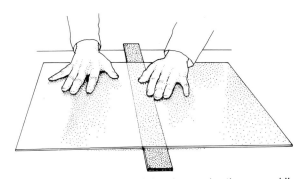

Fig. 25 Placing the metal straightedge under the scored line n the glass and pressing down gently with the flat of the hands to snap the glass cleanly

Glass tends to deform with age and it might be marginally thicker in one area than another. This can have an effect on how easily the glass snaps cleanly. If you use new glass, made with modern production methods, you have a better chance of starting off with a sheet of even thickness.

Sealing in the glass

Once you have cut the glass, drop it into the frame. In conservation framing the next stage is to seal it into the rebate. This stops anything getting at your picture from the front. There are three main dangers in this respect. The first, and most obvious, are tiny insects called thunder flies, which delight in crawling in behind the glass and dying all over the front of your picture. The second, slightly less obvious danger, is the spring-cleaner who wipes down all the pictures with a wet cloth. The water collects at the bottom of the frame and is readily sucked up behind the glass and on to the painting. You should use very little moisture when you clean the glass on framed pictures. It is tempting to give them a good spray with a proprietary glass cleaner and then wipe them dry. However, most of these cleaners contain soap, or a solvent, which helps to remove grease or dirt. Over a period of time they will manage to seep under the rebate and behind the glass, even when the glass has been sealed in with tape. The last danger is one that you will not be aware of until it is much too late. Even the cleanest house has pollutants in the atmosphere, such as sulphur from coal or gas fires, cigarette smoke, or just the car exhaust fumes from the road outside. These can cause irreparable damage to your works of art. Best to seal them out in the first place.

This can easily be done using the brown gum tape that is sold in most stationers. Cut four strips to fit inside the rebate of your frame. Use a damp sponge to moisten lightly first the paper side of the tape and then the glue. This makes the tape more flexible and easier to press down into the frame. Use the tape to seal the gap between the edge of the glass and the inside of the frame (**fig. 26**). As you slide the tape against the glass it will inevitably smear the glass with wet glue so wait until everything is dry and then give the glass a good clean on both sides.

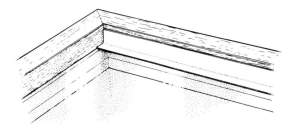

Fig. 26 Taping the glass in the rebate with brown gum tape or white framer's tape

Other forms of glazing

The combination of a dark painting and poor lighting can make the glazing in a frame act like a mirror so that you are disturbed by your own reflection when you try to view the work. To avoid this some museums and galleries use non-reflecting glass. Although this has been treated so that it reflects less light, it will still reflect a small amount and with some makes this reflection, especially of strong, directional light from spotlights, can have a green or purplish cast. This reflection does not affect the colours of the picture, however. All non-reflecting glass is quite expensive and usually has to be ordered specially. If you are determined to use it then let the glazier cut and fit it for you.

Some of you may have heard of museums and art galleries also using Perspex or Plexiglass for glazing. This is a transparent plastic sheet which is very stable and does not seem to deteriorate in any way over long periods of time. Museums use it mainly for pictures which are sent out on loan because, unlike glass, it does not break. It does, however, have some disadvantages. It can scratch very easily and also builds up a static charge, so it cannot be used over powdery materials such as pastels. In addition to this it is not as rigid as glass and will bow in over large paintings and touch the picture unless a large space is left in the frame between the glazing and the work. It is a lot more expensive than glass and not as easily available.

If you do decide to use it, buy the 4 mm (⅛ in) thickness since anything thinner is too flimsy to be of much use. You can cut it to size with a saw and will need to

use a good-quality pressure-sensitive tape, such as 3M Magic Tape, to seal it into the frame.

Fig. 27 shows three pictures which have been glazed in different ways. The top picture has ordinary glass, the photograph above has non-reflecting glass, and the picture opposite is glazed with Perspex.

g. 27 The watercolour portrait (*left*) has been glazed with
rmal picture glass; the Edwardian art photograph (*below*
t) has been glazed with non-reflecting glass; and the
stract landscape (*below*) has been glazed with Perspex

BACKBOARDS

Finally we come to the last side of our frame. Some commercial framers will omit the backboard as a cost-cutting exercise. They put the work of art in the frame and seal over the back with a sheet of brown paper. However, a backboard is an essential part of the frame and no-one could claim to be doing conservation framing if they left it out. A backboard seals the artwork into its protective box. If this isn't done, all of the dangers you have so carefully kept out at the front by taping in the glazing can quite simply go round and get in at the back. This includes some of our large insect friends.

Unless you hang your pictures in an air-conditioned environment they will experience daily and seasonal changes in temperature and humidity. This applies to your home and quite a few art galleries. Conservation scientists have established that a large percentage of the damage suffered by paintings or sculptures is caused by these constant changes. They can cause any work of art on paper to wrinkle and deform. The canvas of an oil or acrylic painting can slacken or tighten, either of which can crack the paint layer. Once you have constructed your frame with glazing and a backboard you will have sealed your picture into its own mini-environment where the temperature and humidity will change only very slowly. This will help to minimize any damage. Lastly, and most importantly, the backboard protects the artwork from any hard knocks.

Choosing the correct material

The backboard needs to be made of a material that is rigid, fairly light, easily cut, water-resistant, available in large sheets, and cheap. Two materials that fit the description are hardboard (Masonite) and polycarbonate sheeting.

Most people will have heard of hardboard. It is made from wood fibres which are compressed into rigid sheets. Standard hardboard will lose its strength over

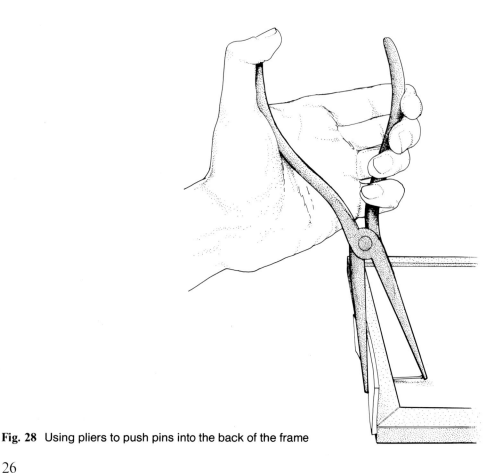

Fig. 28 Using pliers to push pins into the back of the frame

everal years and will need to be checked at regular intervals. Tempered hardboard, which is made by soaking standard hardboard with oils and resins, will last for much longer. It also has greater moisture resistance. Perhaps its one drawback is that it is heavier, and usually thicker, than standard hardboard and is therefore harder to cut. Hardboard usually has one smooth side and one rough. Use it with the smooth side out on the frame. It collects less dust this way.

Polycarbonate sheeting is one of those modern materials which can be seen all around you, although you may not have noticed it. It is a plastic sheet constructed rather like a double-sided corrugated board. Take a closer look at the next estate agent's board you come across. If it looks faintly lined then it is probably made of polycarbonate. Because this is water-resistant and fairly weather-resilient it is often used as the backing for outdoor advertisements, and because it has a double thickness it is surprisingly resistant to hard knocks. You might have to buy it in full-sized sheets, but you can cut it to size with a sharp knife.

I think I should give a few examples here of materials that you should *not* use for backboards. First of all you should not use wood. If this is untreated – and backboards are usually plain, unvarnished pieces of wood or plywood – it will contain resinous materials which can leach out of the wood and on to the back of the artwork. It is not uncommon to remove a wooden backboard from a watercolour and find the pattern of the wood grain burnt into the back of the paper. I have already mentioned the unsuitability of using brown paper in place of a backboard. In the same way you should not use any paper board or card. They have little or no water resistance.

Fitting the backboard

When you have chosen your material, simply measure the inside rebate of the frame in the same way as for the glass and cut the backboard to size so that it fits snugly inside the frame. It will then have to be fixed into the back of the frame. You can use panel pins or veneer pins for this. Hammering them home is possible, but often results in tiny fragments of dust getting knocked into the frame and on to the front of the artwork. This can be exasperating. Just when you think you have finished, you turn the frame round to admire the picture and find it covered with flecks. To avoid this, if I am using pins I squeeze them in with pliers (**fig. 28**). You should put a small piece of card between the pliers and the outside of the frame otherwise you can bruise the moulding when you apply the pressure.

Most commercial framers use a gun rather like a staple gun, which fires diamond- or triangular-shaped pieces of metal into the back of the frame to hold the backboard in place (**fig. 29**). I used to hate these since I

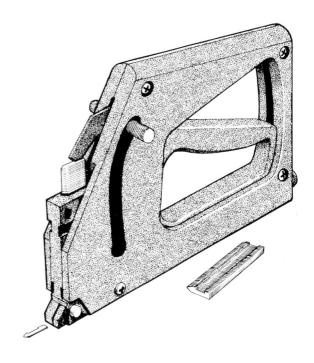

Fig. 29 A framer's gun which fires metal points into the back of the moulding to hold the backboard in place

mainly came across them when I was taking frames apart in order to treat the pictures and they can be very sharp on the fingers when you are not expecting them. However, I have been converted recently by their speed and efficiency, and the initial outlay has been more than covered by the time I have saved in not having to dismantle the picture several times to get rid of flecks. Be warned, though, that great force is used to fire the metal piece into the frame and this will be more than enough to loosen the corners of the moulding if they are not firmly secured. To help prevent this, stand the frame on its edge on a firm surface such as a table top and fire the metal fastener down into the back of the moulding so that the table takes the shock.

Whichever method you use to secure the backboard you should then seal the gap between the edges of the backboard and the frame with brown gum tape. This not only neatens the whole thing but will also prevent any insects, dust or other debris entering the frame from the back.

At this point you have finished learning about the basic frame so it might be a good idea to review what we have covered so far. You now know how to choose, mitre, pin and glue the moulding for your frame. You know about different kinds of glazing and how to cut the glass for your frame. You know about backboards and how to secure them. As well as this I hope you are beginning to understand some of the reasoning behind conservation framing and how it can help to protect and preserve your works of art.

FRAMING WATERCOLOURS

Now that you know how to make a frame you can use it to frame a watercolour. This kind of framing can be used for any simple work of art on paper. I shall deal with special cases later on.

Those of you who sometimes visit country houses might have come across a family print room. Painting and drawing were considered ladylike accomplishments in the last century and most of the women who lived in these great houses would have been expected at least to attempt watercolour painting. The best pictures would be arranged nicely and stuck on the walls of a small sitting room. They were often given frames of cut paper or lace, which would be stuck to the wall around them. Sometimes the family would add prints or drawings to the collection on the walls. Another method of keeping and displaying works of art on paper was to stick them into albums. A few drawings would be framed and hung.

Choosing mount board

It has been traditional for the last two centuries to enclose a work of art on paper in a window mount when it is framed. For conservation framing it is essential to use a mount. There are probably as man different kinds of mount board on the market a there are mouldings, but only some can be used safely You may have noticed that I have started to use th term 'board' for what most people might refer to a cardboard. It is important to be aware of the differ ences. When paper reaches a certain thickness or i laminated together in sheets it becomes board. Card board is literally the board used to make greeting cards or playing cards. If you hear someone refer t their mount board as card you should begin to wonde if they know what they are talking about!

A mount for a print or drawing is made of two parts: backing board and a front piece which has a bevelle aperture. These are hinged together down their longes edge so that they open like a book (**fig. 30**). As you ca see, the work of art is hinged inside the window moun which closes over it. The picture is viewed through th opening in the front board. In this way the window mount protects the picture and because of this it i vitally important that the materials of the mount ar very pure. If the window mount deteriorates in any wa it will affect the artwork.

For a long time almost all of the board on the mark was made of the cheapest material available with n thought to its long-term use. This kind of board ha three distinct features. It has a front surface, a middl layer and a back surface. These three parts can loo very different. The front surface is quite often a sheet coloured paper. The middle layer is made of cheapl produced wood fibres, which are usually very acidi have poor strength, and start to deteriorate quickly. Th back surface is another sheet of paper, often very thi which is laminated over the middle layer to hide th coarseness of the fibres.

These boards quite simply break down over a matte of years – in the worst cases, months – and produc acids and other dangerous substances which will bur into the work of art. They also become very fragile an instead of protecting the picture they end up weake than the painting itself. The bevelled edge of the aper ture in the window mount starts off as a white or crean line but, as the middle layer deteriorates, it slowly turn yellow or brown. Often, when this has happened, a yel low or brown line will also be burnt into the front of th artwork where the edge of the bevel touches it. Puttin something precious, either in financial terms or of sen timental value, next to one of these boards is practicall the same as tearing it up and throwing it away. Abou

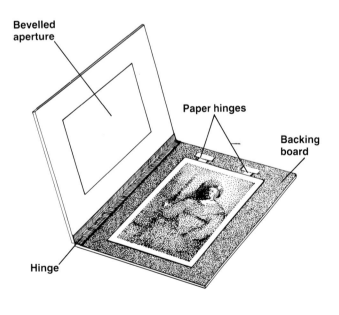

Fig. 30 The parts of a window mount

Bevelled aperture

Paper hinges

Backing board

Hinge

Fig. 31 A selection of conservation-quality mount boards

alf of my time as a conservator is spent in repairing ¹e damage caused by this kind of acidic mount board.

Obviously, when paper conservators realized what ⁻as causing so much of the damage they insisted on ⁻nding a board which was safe, longer lasting, and ⁻hich would not harm the work of art. For many years ⁻ has been possible to buy conservation-quality board,

but only by ordering directly from the manufacturers or importers and then only in large quantities. Unless by chance your framer stocked some of this board you would not have been able to buy it.

Luckily, this has all changed and it is now possible to buy conservation-quality mount board in art shops and framing suppliers (**fig. 31**). If you are doing

conservation framing you must use Conservation Board or Museum Board. Conservation Board is the standard conservation-quality board and should be used as a matter of course. Museum Board is slightly more expensive to produce and therefore costs more to buy. It is usually thicker and is made of extremely pure materials. It is used by museums and art galleries to protect valuable works of art. There are also special cases where it should definitely be used in preference to Conservation Board. I shall cover these in the chapter on framing photographs (see page 44).

Fig. 32 shows a watercolour which has suffered badly from poor mount materials and poor framing practices. It is stuck to a piece of board which is made of acidic materials. In this case the disfiguring brown marks, called foxing, are caused by a specific mould which flourishes in acidic conditions. There was no front window to the mount and the watercolour was pushed up against the glass, which was not sealed against dust. This has resulted in a thin layer of dirt covering the front of the watercolour. The faint brown line just above the girl's head is caused by the wooden

Fig. 32 (*left*) This picture shows the results of poor mounting and framing (*photo*: David J. Clarke)

Fig. 33 (*below*) After restoration the picture has been hinged into a Conservation Board window mount with Japanese paper hinges (*photo*: David J. Clarke)

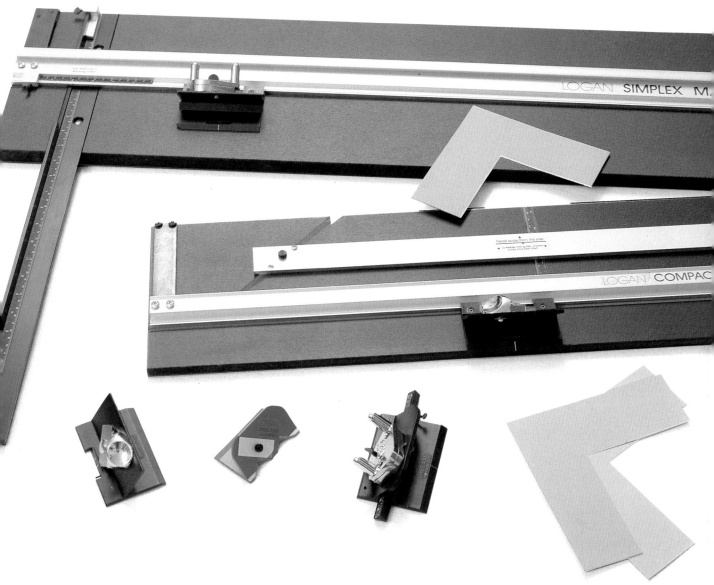

Fig. 34 A selection of mount cutters. The three small ones at the front are perfectly adequate if you are cutting only the occasional mount and the two large ones at the back are sturdy enough for professional mount cutting

backboard of the frame: the resinous materials in the wood have burnt through the backing board and on to the front of the picture.

This watercolour needed long, careful restoration treatment. After the results of the poor mount board and bad framing were removed the picture was mounted into a Museum Board mount (**fig. 33**). The use of carefully chosen, conservation-quality materials should mean that it will be preserved in a good condition for many years.

Cutting a mount

Machines called mount cutters, which cut the bevelled opening in the mount, come in all shapes and sizes (**fig. 34**). I find some of them easy to use and others not.

On the other hand, different people find they can cut mounts simply and easily with cutters that I can never manage. It is all a matter of trying out several different ones until you find a mount cutter you like and whose foibles match your own. Daler-Rowney's Logan Compact mount cutter is a good one to choose if you intend to cut window mounts frequently.

Like everything else it would be sensible for you to practice on a cheap piece of board before you try cutting the more expensive Conservation Board. Don't worry too much about achieving perfection right away. Have a look at what everyone else manages. I usually find myself doing this at art exhibitions, especially of Minimal Art. Everyone thinks you are deep in contemplation of the artist's work when in fact you are checking to see if he has any overcuts on his window mounts.

Measuring up When you come to cut your mount, first measure the inside rebate size of your frame and deduct about 2 mm (1/16 in) from the height and width in the same way that you measured up for your glass and backboard. Once again you want the mount to fit snugly inside the frame. Make sure you write down clearly which is the height measurement and which is the width. If you get them confused the mount will not fit the picture after you have cut the aperture.

Next measure the height and width of the sight size of your picture. Write these measurements under the frame measurements and subtract one from the other.

Let's deal with the width of the margins first. If the picture is to be in the middle of the board then the margins of mount board at either side must be exactly the same, so all you have to do here is divide the width measurement by two. Write this figure in the width column. This is the measurement you will use to cut your mount.

Now for the height. This is a little more difficult. If you make the mount the same size both above and below the picture it will look wrong. It is an optical illusion, but the picture will appear to be too far down in the mount. To counteract this the bottom measurement must be slightly larger than the top, by about 5–10 mm (1/4–3/8 in). Write these two measurements down in the height column. You should have three measurements

now – one for the top margin of your mount, one for the bottom margin, and one for both of the sides. Don worry if this seems a bit confusing at the momen **Fig. 35** shows an example of how these measuremen are worked out. Copy this and put in your own figure This sort of calculation gets easier with practice. If yo get into the habit of doing it logically, step by step, yo will make fewer mistakes.

Cutting the opening Cut your piece of board to th inside rebate size and drop it face down into the fram to check that it fits snugly. If you need to trim it slightl then remeasure it and change the figures in your calcu lations accordingly. Decide which is going to be the to edge of your board and write TOP on the back of you mount board. Lightly pencil in your top, bottom an side measurements in their proper places on the bac of the board. Use only a soft pencil for writing o the mount board. If you are really tidy an professional about your work you will rub off all th annotations before you use the mount, even thoug they are on the inside and don't show. If you write i ink, however, not only is it irremovable, it might offs on to the margins of your painting.

Most mount cutters cut the opening from the bac so you will be able to check your measurements a you go along. All mount cutters use slightly, or eve

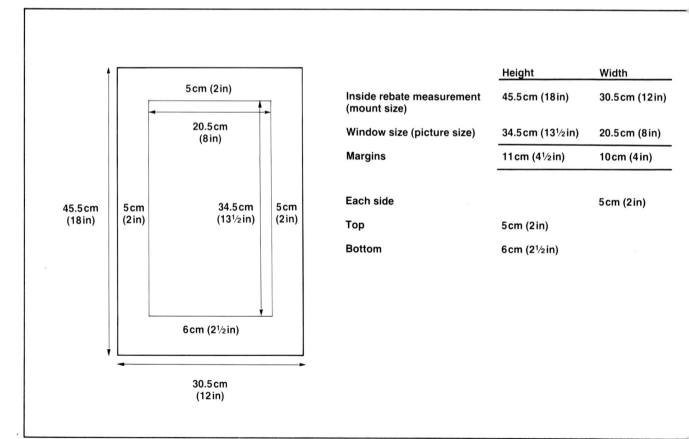

	Height	Width
Inside rebate measurement (mount size)	45.5 cm (18 in)	30.5 cm (12 in)
Window size (picture size)	34.5 cm (13½ in)	20.5 cm (8 in)
Margins	11 cm (4½ in)	10 cm (4 in)
Each side		5 cm (2 in)
Top	5 cm (2 in)	
Bottom	6 cm (2½ in)	

Fig. 35 Working out the mount measurements

rastically, different procedures to cut mounts. I have used the Daler-Rowney Logan Compact mount cutter here to show you how a window mount is cut. The instructions given might not apply to another make of cutter, so you should check with the manufacturer's instructions before you begin. All mount cutters work on the same basic idea, that of cutting four straight lines, with bevelled edges, through the board. If you are using this mount cutter, or a very similar one, then follow the illustrations in **figs. 36–39**.

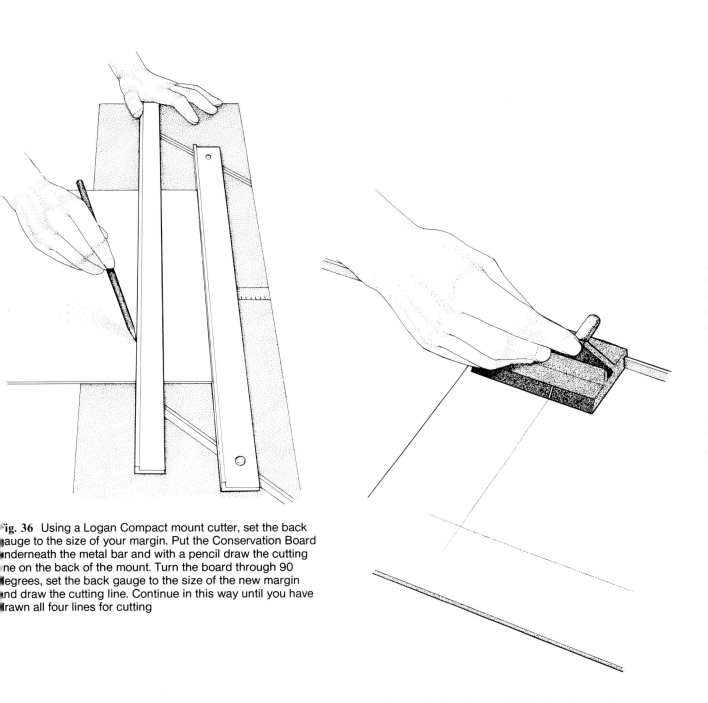

Fig. 36 Using a Logan Compact mount cutter, set the back gauge to the size of your margin. Put the Conservation Board underneath the metal bar and with a pencil draw the cutting line on the back of the mount. Turn the board through 90 degrees, set the back gauge to the size of the new margin and draw the cutting line. Continue in this way until you have drawn all four lines for cutting

Fig. 37 Start with the side margin. Position the cutting head on the front bar. Set the back gauge for the side margin measurement. Place the board under the front bar with the top edge on the left side and line up the cutting head so that the silver mark on its side is level with the pencil line for the top margin. Push the blade into the board and slide the head along the front bar towards the pencil line for the bottom margin

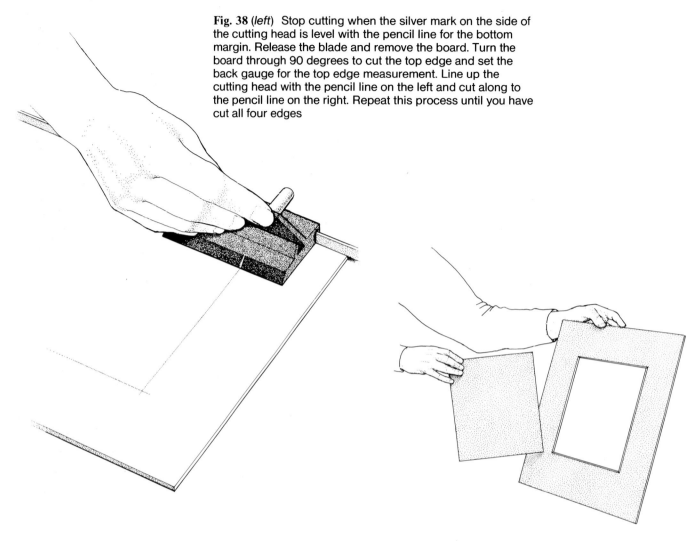

Fig. 38 (*left*) Stop cutting when the silver mark on the side of the cutting head is level with the pencil line for the bottom margin. Release the blade and remove the board. Turn the board through 90 degrees to cut the top edge and set the back gauge for the top edge measurement. Line up the cutting head with the pencil line on the left and cut along to the pencil line on the right. Repeat this process until you have cut all four edges

Fig. 39 When you have made four cuts the middle of the board can be removed, leaving you with the bevelled window mount

Once you have cut the window, and before you go any further, check against your picture that the window is the right size. The most common mistake is to cut a window mount which is of a landscape format – that is, wider than it is tall – for a picture which is of a portrait format – that is, taller than it is wide. This happens when you get your height and width measurements mixed up.

You must now cut a second piece of Conservation Board, which will fit behind your picture and make the other half of your mount, but first I had better explain why you need it. After all, you can't see this part of the mount and you might think that if you leave it out no-one will ever know. However, it is one of the basic rules in conservation framing that any work of art on paper should touch only Conservation Board. The aim is to cocoon your work in acid-free board in order to protect it. You will remember that I have already mentioned

the damage done to prints and drawings by atmospheric pollution or changes in the temperature and moisture in the air. Conservation and Museum Board are so pure that they soak up any minute changes of impurities before they can get to your artwork to cause damage. The more acid-free board you can pack into your frame, the better protection it can give.

Cut a slightly larger piece of Conservation Board for the backing board and trim it to size, using the front window mount as a guide. Then hinge the window mount to the backing board down the longest edge. Use brown gum paper as a hinge or, better still, white acid-free linen tape. Do not use any self-adhesive tape inside the mount. Not only do these tapes dry out and fall off, the adhesive on them has a tendency to creep. This means that it softens with age and spreads out from under the plastic strip. It can stain and irreparably damage your artwork.

Plastic bevels While I am writing about cutting bevelled openings in mount board you might be interested in a new product on the market. These are coloured plastic strips which clip over the edges of the opening in the front mount and give the effect of a coloured bevel (**fig. 40**). They can look quite pretty with differently coloured Conservation Board.

If you use these you do not need to cut a bevelled opening in the board; simply use a sharp knife to make the window. The plastic strips need to have mitred corners in order to fit neatly into the rectangular opening. You could try using your mitre box to cut them or, better still, ask the retailer if he will cut and mitre them for you. I am not sure how the plastic itself will age or what effect it might have on the work of art inside the frame, so if you do want to use these strips, don't put them in with the family heirlooms.

Fig. 40 (*right* and *below*) Using plastic bevels to add a line of contrasting colour to the aperture in the window mount (*photos*: courtesy of Daler-Rowney)

Hinging a watercolour

On first sight it might seem that hinging your print, drawing or watercolour into the Conservation Board window mount is one of the easiest parts of the whole process, but be warned; if I spend half my time dealing with the damaging effects of acidic mount board I must spend the other half trying to reverse the ravages caused by the wrong hinging materials.

It costs money to produce a glue or adhesive which will last for years. Many of the products that we take for granted are really quite new and their manufactu[re] goes back only a decade or two. Many people, especially art students it seems, use masking tape to hing[e] their pictures. This tape was originally designed for th[e] car industry. The manufacturers stuck lines of it alon[g] the cars so that it masked the original paint and the[y] could spray decorative strips on the sides of th[e] vehicles. When the paint was dry the tape was remove[d]. In fact, those of you who paint in acrylics will know tha[t] this tape is still very useful for masking areas [of] underpainting when a hard-edged shape is required o[n] top. The tape was never designed to last, however. As [it] ages the adhesive turns yellow and it will stain an[y] paper with which it is in contact. After about a year th[e] yellow stain is virtually impossible to remove.

Fig. 41 Japanese paper and methyl cellulose paste should be used to hinge the most valuable items. Acid-free framer's tape is perfectly adequate for everything else

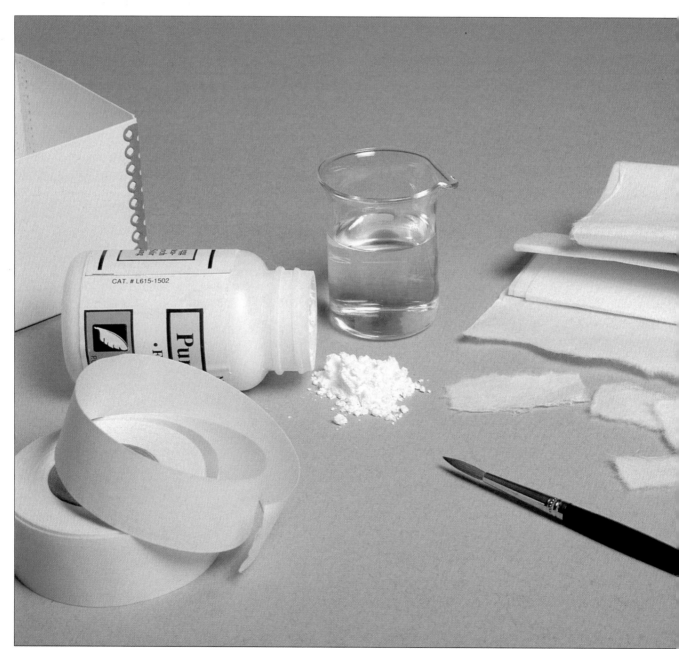

Think back to the last paperback book you saw which had been repaired with pressure-sensitive tape. The chances are that it was yellow and stained. The same will happen to your work of art if you use the wrong materials. This kind of tape was probably designed to secure parcels. Again, it was certainly not designed to last. On average I must get a telephone call or a visit once a month from some desperate artist or illustrator who is having an exhibition of his work and who has looked back through his portfolios only to find that much of his early work is badly marked with old adhesive stains.

The correct materials to use In my job as a paper conservator I must have come across hinges made of everything sticky known to man, from surgical tape to sealing wax. A simple rule of thumb is that all of the tapes and glues you can buy over the counter in your local shop will probably damage your painting. This is the one occasion you will have to go to a supplier of conservation-standard materials. You can use either the white gum paper tape called framer's tape, which has an acid-free paper backing and a starch-based adhesive, or, for a more professional job, use Japanese paper and methyl cellulose paste. Japanese paper, as its name implies, is made in Japan. It is a thin, strong, flexible tissue. You might have come across decorative Japanese papers in shops. They usually have lace patterns in them, or bits of flowers and leaves. Save these kinds of paper for wrapping birthday presents. Do *not* use them for hinges. You need the thin, plain sheets of paper. Conservators use these because they are made with very long paper fibres, which means they can be carefully torn to give a feathered edge. When this is tuck behind the artwork as a hinge it does not show through on to the front as a hard line.

Because I use so much I have to buy these materials in large amounts and up to now that was the only way to find them. Recently, however, they have been marketed in small amounts especially for the home market (**fig. 41**). I suggest you ask about them in your local art suppliers or framing shop. Be persistent!

The different methods of hinging I am going to cover two main methods of hinging here but first I had better mention one that is quite commonly used commercially but which is generally wrong for a valuable work of art. This is when the picture is totally stuck to a piece of mount board, a process that is variously called laminating or dry-mounting. The result is a piece of paper that is completely flat. Now as I sit at my desk writing this I am surrounded by pieces of paper – letters, telephone bills, receipts – and none of them is flat. All paper moves constantly, however slightly, and this includes paintings and drawings. If you stick your picture down absolutely flat, not only will you have made it look like a table mat but you will have stored up trouble for the future if ever you want to get if off again.

All paper conservators must have clients, dealers or collectors who come to them with a print or drawing they have picked up in a sale, usually very cheap, which they know is valuable. The only trouble is that it seems to be dry-mounted very firmly to its backing board. Can it be removed? Unless they are very lucky the answer is usually no. The only thing they can hope to do is put the work back into its frame and try to sell it, hoping nobody will notice. Which is presumably why it was so cheap in the first place.

So, paper is usually hinged by the top edge and allowed to expand and contract normally. The hinges are always stuck on the back. You should never alter the appearance of a painting by sticking something on the front, or writing annotations down the side, or even indicating the extent of the window mount with pencil lines. This is especially true if the painting was done by someone else; most people would agree that it is wrong to interfere with the intention of an artist's work. But what about your own work? After all, you are in the best position to decide what should be shown, surely? All artists assume this and yet it is heart-breaking to dismantle a beautiful Victorian watercolour and find an extra part of the composition hidden under the mount which has been ruined by someone writing the framing instructions on it. Give future generations the chance to decide how they want to display your work.

Figs. 42–44 show how to make a T-hinge, a folded hinge, and a float mount, respectively. The first one is the strongest and should always be used if the edges of the painting are hidden under the window mount (**fig. 42**). Even though only a small amount of the actual hinge is attached to the artwork the weight of the picture is spread over a much larger area by the T-bar on the top. The second hinge is still a very strong joint and

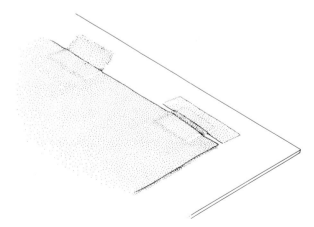

Fig. 42 Tear out a strip of Japanese paper or use a small hinge of framer's tape and stick it to the back of the picture. Let it dry under a weight. Attach the picture to the backing board with a cross piece of framer's tape

Fig. 43 To hide the hinges, after you have attached them to the back of the picture, fold the top edge of the hinge underneath and attach the picture to the backing board with a piece of framer's tape

Fig. 44 If you want the edges of the picture to show, use folded hinges in all four corners. The dotted lines in the illustration indicate the position of the hinges on the back of the picture

the reinforcing strip underneath it will stop it peeling away from the backing board (**fig. 43**). If you want all the edges of the paper to show, however, you must cut the aperture large enough so that the paper 'floats' inside the space. In this case, hinge it down using the folded hinges, but also slip two small folds of hinging paper under the bottom corners (**fig. 44**). If you forget to do this, when you have finished framing your picture the paper will swing forwards inside the frame and the bottom edge will end up resting against the glass.

Using Conservation Board slips

Perhaps at this point I should say a few words about works of art touching the glazing. The most logical and obvious method of keeping a piece of paper flat and holding it in place in the frame would seem to be by sandwiching it between the glass and the backboard but there are several reasons why this should not be done. First of all, over the passage of time the picture can quite simply stick to the glass, especially if it is a photograph. There is no simple way to remove a photograph which has stuck firmly to the glazing. I know; I have tried. My last experience of this was a large, Victorian photograph of a client's grandmother as a child. It had been framed against non-reflecting glass and large patches of the photographic emulsion were firmly stuck to the glazing. In fact, the black and white image had torn away from the photographic paper and there was nothing I could do to save it.

The second reason is that, in certain conditions, tiny amounts of moisture can form on the inside of the glass. These will stain the picture and probably encourage it to develop mould. Mould growth on a painting can be quite spectacular. Often it is little more than a light dusting of black spores. Occasionally, however, it turns into brightly coloured pink, green or blue patches. The effects of these moulds are difficult, if not impossible, to remove.

The final reason for not squeezing your picture between the backboard and the glazing is that the smooth surface of the glass can polish the surface of the picture, especially if this has thickly painted impasto areas.

When a window mount is used these problems are prevented as it holds the work away from the glass; but what should you do if you want to display your picture without a front window mount? In this case you should cut a Conservation Board backing board to fit the frame and hinge your work to it as before. You can then cut thin strips of Conservation Board just slightly narrower than the front rebate of your frame and tap them in behind the glass so that they are hidden from sight by the front rebate (**fig. 45**). The Conservation Board backing board will rest against these so that your picture is held away from the glass.

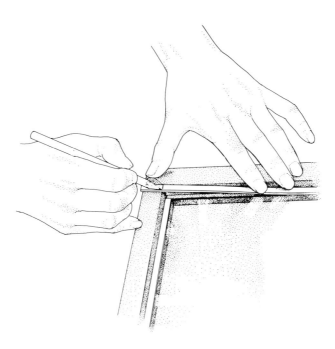

Fig. 45 Measuring and fitting slips of Conservation Board behind the glazing to hold the picture away from the glass

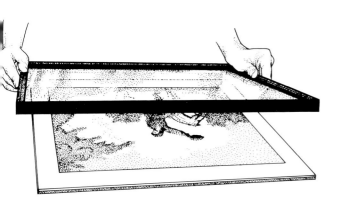

Fig. 46 Lowering the frame and glazing over the picture

Fig. 47 Turning the whole frame over in order to pin the backboard

Fitting the picture

Well, you have made the frame and hinged your picture into its Conservation Board window mount. Let's now put the two together.

Place the backboard flat on your work surface and lay the picture, in its mount, face up on it. Make sure that the glass in the frame is scrupulously clean and that there are no bits of dust lurking in the corners. Lower the frame on top of the picture, checking through the glass that there are no flecks, stray hairs or dust getting trapped inside on top of the picture (**fig. 46**). You will need patience at this stage: lowering the frame on top of the picture seems to attract all sorts of dust and debris from the atmosphere. When you are convinced that the inside of the frame is dust free, grip the frame and backboard firmly in both hands and turn the whole lot over so that the frame is face down (**fig. 47**). Pin in the backboard as described earlier (see page 27) and seal it with brown gum tape. When this has dried, turn the frame over and take a few moments to stand back and admire your handiwork.

HANGING FITTINGS

These are many and varied and will have to be chosen to suit your particular frame, but as far as conservation framing is concerned, the main rule is that the hanging fittings should be attached to your frame by screwing or pinning them into the back rebate of the moulding. Do not use hanging fittings that are attached to the backboard. If you are using a polycarbonate backboard they will be ripped out by the weight of the picture. Hardboard backboards are another matter and you will often see commercial framing where the hanging fitting is attached to this kind of backboard. This is usually because the back rebate of the moulding is so thin and inadequate that it would be impossible to screw anything into it without splitting the wood. If you have chosen a conservation-standard moulding in the first place you should not have this problem. As I mentioned earlier, standard-quality hardboard loses its strength quite quickly; I have come across frames where the hanging fittings have simply been torn out as the hardboard weakened. Tempered hardboard is too thick and tough for most of these kinds of fittings.

Perhaps the main objection to any kind of hanging fitting attached to the backboard is that eventually it will push into the back of the painting. At the very best this causes lumps and bumps inside the frame, which transfer themselves on to the mount backing board and distort the artwork. At the very worst they can protrude on to the front of the picture itself.

Fig. 48 shows a variety of hanging fittings, which can be divided into three groups: the parts that are screwed into the frame; the parts that are pinned into the wall; and the chains and wires that are used for hanging the pictures. If you can pick up your frame with one hand without straining any muscles then you will probably get away with using simple eyelet screws and wire for hanging it at home. Eyelet screws come in a variety of sizes; choose ones that will support the weight of your frame but will not split the wood when you screw them into the back of the moulding.

You should attach all fittings about two thirds of the way up the sides of the frame. Unless you are using mirror plates the fittings will protrude slightly from the back of the frame and cause it to lean away from the wall when you hang it. The nearer the fittings are to the top of the frame, the less it will lean. If you put them too near the top edge, however, the hanging wire will be visible when the picture is on the wall.

For preference, use picture hangers' stranded metal wire, which is also illustrated in **fig. 48**. Do not use string; it breaks. Thick cord is better, but it slow stretches with the weight of the frame and you will hav to retie it at regular intervals. It is much neater an more professional if the hanging wires do not sho above the frame.

The long, thin hooks with two or three countersun screw holes illustrated in **fig. 48** should be used if yo are hanging large pictures with chains. Once agai they should be screwed firmly into the moulding. I hav also included in the illustration some traditional pic ture hooks, which hook over a picture rail. Personally, would use these only if I were hanging heavy picture on brass chains, and then I would use two, level wit the sides of the frame and with two parallel lengths c chain attached to them.

If you are hanging a lighter picture with hooks an wire you can, of course, simply bang a nail into the wa and hang it from that. A neater, and probably more pe manent way, is to use the picture hook with angled pir shown in the illustration. These have either one pin fc small frames or two for slightly heavier ones. For hang ing pictures on a solid brick wall you will need to us the white, hard-wall hooks.

If you want your frame to lie flat against the wall, c you are worried about security, you should use mirrc plates to hang your pictures. These are shaped met plates with three countersunk screw holes in them. Th flat edge of the plate is lined up with the inside edge c your moulding so that the curved part protrudes abov the edge of the frame. The plate is screwed in plac using the two screw holes. The frame is then attached t the wall by screwing through the third hole in th curved part of the plate.

Finally, I have included in the illustration som examples of the kinds of fittings which are normall attached to the backboard. If these are the only fitting you can find, don't despair. You can pin or screw then into the moulding like the others and use them wit framer's wire.

Framing for exhibitions

If you are framing your paintings for an exhibition check with the gallery on the kinds of hanging fitting they allow. Most galleries are very fussy about havin holes knocked in their walls. You will want to spend a the time allotted in arranging your works to their bes advantage rather than dashing around trying to fin special hooks.

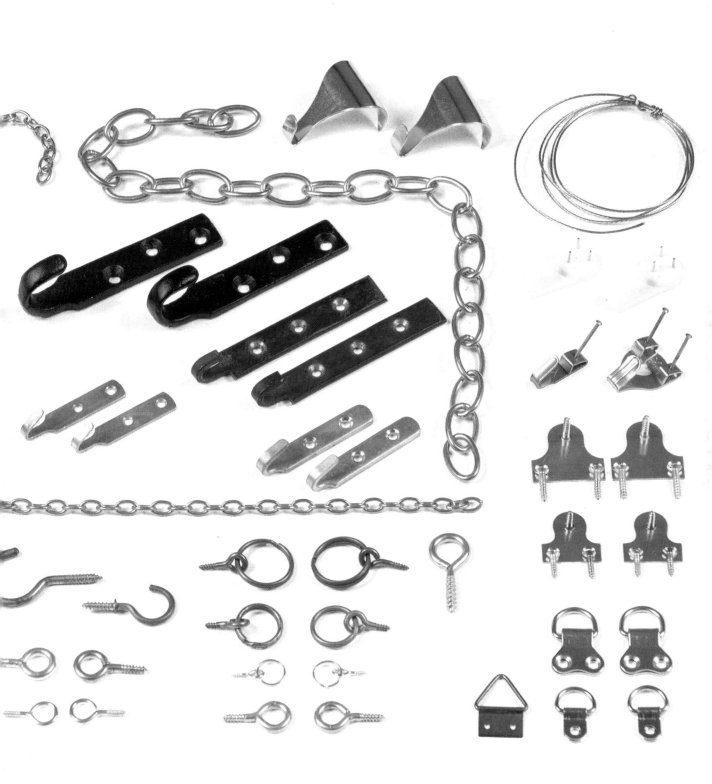

Fig. 48 A selection of hanging fittings

FRAMING PASTELS

Although this chapter is specifically about pastel paintings, the information covered here also applies to any drawing done with a friable medium. This includes drawings done with chalks, charcoal and conté crayon.

Paintings in all of these different media, and especially pastel, need special treatment when they are framed. A stick of pastel is simply ground pigment held together by very little adhesive. The small amount of pressure applied when moving it across the surface of a piece of paper is enough to cause the stick to break up and leave a drawn line. Some of the smallest specks of pigment are trapped in the paper fibres but most of the pastel sits on the surface. It is quite easily dislodged. Fixing the pastel can help, but this should be done with care. If you usually fix your pastel drawings, either while you are working on them or when you have finished, Daler-Rowney's Perfix spray fixative is probably one of the safest to use. Most of the other fixatives tend to yellow over a period of time and the ones based on shellac are especially difficult to remove. I would advise against fixing an old pastel painting. If you are worried about it you should take it to a conservator for advice.

Even if you have fixed your work of art it is important that a pastel painting never comes into contact with the glazing otherwise the pastel will offset on to the back of the glass. For this reason most pastel drawings and paintings need quite a deep frame. You should either cut a window mount or insert slips of Conservation Board behind the glass to hold the paper away from it. Look back to the chapter on framing a watercolour to see how this is done (see page 38). The larger the painting, the deeper the slips or window mount must be so that you can be absolutely sure that the work of art will not bow outwards and touch the glass. Any pastel painting that is larger than the size of this book, especially if the pastel is thickly applied, should have a double window mount, or at least 5 mm (¼ in) thick slips inserted behind the glass.

Double window mounts

A double window mount can look really professional. Start by cutting a normal-sized window in your front board, showing off the picture to its best advantage. The next stage is a real test of your mount-cutting skill. Cut a second board the same size as the first and cut the window in this board 5 mm (¼ in) larger all round. Let's say, for example, that the aperture in your first board measures 250 × 200 mm (10 × 8 in); the opening in your second board should therefore measure 260 × 210 mm (10½ × 8½ in). Position the second board over the first, making sure that they are both perfectly evenly aligned, and you will be able to see the thin border of the first mount through the window of the second. Fix the two boards together at the corners with tiny tabs of double-sided pressure-sensitive tape between them (**fig. 49**). Hinge this double window mount to the conservation backing board in the usual way and use this special mount to protect your picture.

If you are cutting double window mounts you could try combinations of the differently coloured Conservation Boards that are available. There is no rule that says both mounts have to be the same colour. Remember, however, what I wrote in the introductory chapter about the dangers of emphasizing some of the colours in a picture to the detriment of the others, and try to combine mount boards in colours that will complement your work rather than fight it. Remember also that the inside board will show only as a thin border around the opening in the top board.

In some of the frames in **fig. 50** the framer has used a gilded fillet to hold the picture away from the glazing. If you decide to do this you must line the back surface of

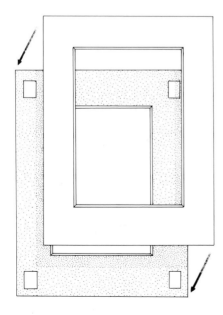

Fig. 49 The top window mount is attached to the bottom window mount with tabs of double-sided tape in the corners

Fig. 50 Wooden fillets have been used as spacers in all of these frames to keep the glazing away from the powdery medium (*photo*: David J. Clarke)

he fillet with strips of Conservation Board before you est the painting against it.

You must always use glass when framing any work of rt done with pastel, charcoal, chalk or conté crayon. 'erspex or Plexiglass, or indeed any kind of plastic

sheeting, should never be used. They all build up static charges when touched, and even if you put a double window mount or thick slips into the frame the chances are that you will end up with your pastel drawing spread thinly and evenly over the back of the glazing.

FRAMING PHOTOGRAPHS

If photographs are to last for any length of time they need special care. More than anything else, photographs are a chemical 'soup' and they can be irreversibly damaged if they are not looked after properly. I shall write a little about exhibiting later, but in this instance it is safe to say that the easiest and quickest way to damage your photographs, especially colour photographs, is to hang them in a strong light, whether it is daylight, sunlight or lamplight.

All of the rules about mounting and framing watercolours and drawings apply here. It is very important that you seal out any atmospheric pollution. There is evidence that even something as innocuous as ordinary household paint drying in the next room can give off fumes that will tarnish your photographs.

If you want to frame your family photographs then using Conservation Board for their mounts is fine. On the other hand, if you are a professional photographer whose photographs are sold as works of art, or you collect important photographs, you should use only Museum Board. In addition, you should buy Museum Board which has passed the silver tarnish test. This is a chemical test used by conservation scientists to see whether the board will slowly give off gases which could cause damage to the photographic image. Most manufacturers will specify this, where appropriate, in their advertising literature.

Hinging techniques for photographs

If you have old photographs which are printed on ordinary photographic paper they can be hinged into your Conservation Board mount ready for framing in the same way as a watercolour. Be very careful when putting water, or anything wet, next to a photograph. The paper tends to expand very quickly when wet and this will not only cause deformations in the picture but might damage the image layer as well. For this reason you would do better to use the framing tape which needs very little moisture to make it stick, rather than Japanese paper and methyl cellulose adhesive.

If your photographs are printed on a modern plastic-coated paper, sometimes called resin-coated paper, you have a problem. The plastic coating is in fact polythene and, as you probably know, nothing sticks to polythene for very long. Even the various masking tapes and

Fig. 51 This collection of framed photographs makes an eye-catching feature in a family living room

pressure-sensitive tapes which appear to stick firmly in place will simply peel away in time, usually leaving a nasty yellow adhesive stain behind them. I occasionally have to treat such photographs – huge works of art which seem to spend their time flying around the world to international exhibitions – and

usually they have come adrift in their mounts because the hinges have peeled off.

One of the safest ways you can avoid this is to attach your photographs to the conservation backing board with photo corners in the same way that you would put them in an album. You will need to cut the opening in

your window mount that little bit smaller on all sides so that the corners will not show when the photograph is in place. Archival-quality photo-mounting corners are available from suppliers of conservation materials (**fig. 52**). The corners shown are generous in depth and if you are mounting small photographs you will have to trim the front edge of the mount corner so that it just clips the front of your photograph and holds it in place.

Please do not feel tempted to use blobs of glue or bits of sticky tape as a temporary measure. Although they

Fig. 52 (*right*) Using archival-quality photo-mounting corners to hinge the family photographs to Conservation Board

Fig. 53 (*below*) For professional mounting, the BEVA 371 adhesive shown under the heated spatula should be used with hinges of Japanese paper (*top*). For everyday photographs archival-quality photo-mounting corners are suitable

ill look as if they have worked, they will not stay in lace for long and the adhesive can still cause an irre-movable stain on your photograph.

Alternative methods of mounting photographs

Most commercial mounters and framers have the equipment for dry-mounting photographs. A thin tis-sue coated on both sides by a heat-seal adhesive is placed between the photograph and the backing board. These are then put into a hot press, which melts the adhesive and sticks the photograph and backing board together under pressure. Irrevocably. The photograph looks nice and flat and the problem of finding an adhe-sive which will stick to it is solved. However, no-one knows how long the adhesive will last and what will happen when it starts to deteriorate. The effect that the changing chemicals in the adhesive might have on the reactive chemicals of the photographic image is any-one's guess.

Some manufacturers claim that their dry-mounting tissue is reversible. Well, it may be; but what you'll have left after you have reversed it is another matter. You might also have difficulty in finding someone willing to reverse this kind of mounting for you, since most of the products blithely recommend reversal methods which entail using copious amounts of chemicals – a situation almost certainly injurious to the conservator's health. I would advise you, therefore, not to use the dry-mount-ing method for photographs that you might want to keep for future generations.

There are, in fact, adhesives on the market which are long-lasting and safe, but they are also very expensive and are sold only in large amounts. They will really only be worth the outlay if you are a professional artist/photographer or a commercial mounter of fine-art

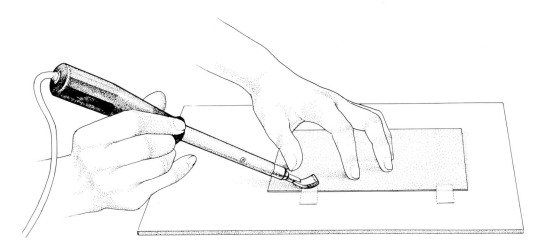

Fig. 54 Using a heated spatula to attach Japanese paper hinges to the back of the photograph with BEVA 371 adhesive

Fig. 55 Completing the hinge with framer's tape or Japanese paper

photographs who needs to know of a reasonably safe, secure method. One such product is BEVA 371, avail-able as an adhesive film which is worth its weight in gold and costs about as much (**fig. 53**). It is readily reversible in white spirit or by being gently reheated.

If you wish to use this method, cut the usual hinges of a strong Japanese paper and, with a thin strip of BEVA 371, tack them to the back of the photograph using a spatula heated to 60°C (140°F), as shown in **fig. 54**. Use the attached hinges to stick the photograph to a Museum Board backing in the usual way with starch paste or methyl cellulose (**fig. 55**).

For the rest of us, who only want our photographs to last long enough to show to the younger generations, using archival-quality photo-mounting corners to attach the pictures to Conservation Board is possibly still the safest and least expensive way to mount them.

FRAMING A WORK ON A STRETCHER

So far we have only considered how to make a frame for a work of art on paper, but you might want to frame a work that is on a stretcher. This is the traditional way to display oil paintings or acrylics on canvas. If you have chosen to paint in oils on a thick board instead of canvas then you can still frame them using this method.

Because the moulding will need to be deeper than usual in order to take the stretcher it will generally be much heavier in appearance on the front as well. However, this need not stop you from being adventurous and trying out non-traditional types of moulding if you wish. There are no hard and fast rules that say a certain moulding must go round a particular kind of picture. Many artists, especially in the last century, painted their pictures and then designed and painted the frames to match. The Pre-Raphaelite painters are a good example of this. Dante Gabriel Rossetti's jewel-like watercolours of medieval and mythical subjects, for instance, were framed in elaborate, gilded frames which were typical examples of the fashion for Victorian Gothic.

If the painting you intend to frame has been varnished you might decide to omit the glazing. The varnish itself will serve as a protective barrier for oil and acrylic paintings. You should, of course, never varnish a work of art on paper. Unlike a work in oils or acrylic, where the varnish sits on the surface of the paint and can usually be removed later if it yellows or cracks, a coat of varnish on a watercolour, print or drawing will simply soak into the paper backing and when it dries it will almost certainly be impossible to remove without damaging the paint layer. If the painting to be framed is one of your own, remember that you must leave any oil painting for several weeks, and preferably months, in order for it to dry completely before you varnish it. The thicker the paint, the longer it takes to dry. If you want to exhibit the painting in a hurry and do not have time to wait, then an application of retouching varnish is a temporary measure; or alternatively, of course, you could glaze it.

I have already explained in the chapter on framing watercolours that a work on paper should not touch the glazing. This also applies to a painting in oils or acrylics. It is especially true if the paint is still not quite dry. In this case, allowing it to come into contact with the glazing will mean that the surface of the paint is flattened and polished, and there is a good chance that it will stick, firmly, to the glazing as it dries.

Care of unglazed pictures Any painting which is hung unglazed for any length of time will gradually get dust and need to be cleaned. Resist the temptation to wipe over with a wet cloth. The paint layer is quite a rigid, inflexible layer compared to the canvas, which can expand and contract with changes in temperature and humidity. This movement is very small but it can result in small cracks in the paint layer itself. If you apply water to the surface of the picture it can be drawn down through these cracks and either cause the canvas to distort or damage the priming layer. Some water-based primers, especially gesso, are very susceptible to water damage. Therefore, if the picture simply has a layer of dust over it, brush it away gently with a soft brush; one of the large Chinese bamboo ones will do.

If the picture belongs to you and the dirt is more serious – a layer of nicotine, for instance, if any members of the family regularly smoke – then you can try cleaning it with barely damp cotton wool swabs. Do not wet the cotton wool by dipping it in a glass of water as this will make it far too wet and you will not be able to control where the water goes on the surface of the picture. In this case the only controlled way to get the swab damp is to suck it. Once it is damp, gently roll the swab across the picture surface. Do not scrub and do not put dirty swabs back in your mouth. If no dirt appears to be coming off by this method then you need expert help. You will also need a trained conservator if your painting has areas of thick paint, or impasto. The dirt gets into the small grooves in the paint strokes and is very difficult to remove. It needs slow, painstaking work, often using a microscope, to clean it out.

If the painting is a large one then the chances are that, even with this gentle method, you will find it very difficult to clean it evenly and again you should be prepared to find a properly trained easel-painting restorer who will have the time and patience to do the job well. This also applies to any oil painting, of whatever size, which is unvarnished, cracked or flaking. You will need specialist help. The best way to avoid all of this trouble is to glaze your paintings in the first place.

Fig. 56 These small oil paintings are all examples of works which can be framed without glazing (*photo*: David J. Clarke

Stretching a canvas

A stretcher is made up of four pieces of wood with the corners shaped so that they fit together to form a rectangle. If the painting is to be more than 0.5 sq. m (about 5 sq. ft) in area then strengthening bars should also be used otherwise the stretcher will bow inwards under the tension of the canvas. Stretchers are reasonably expensive but it is worth while buying them from a reputable manufacturer rather than cutting costs. I do not suggest you even attempt to construct your own. The pieces need to fit together quite precisely or the stretcher will damage the canvas, and eventually the picture.

Most people buy their canvases ready-stretched, but for the hardy souls who like to do everything for themselves the method of stretching a canvas is described here. This technique is also required if you want to display a piece of needlework (see also page 58).

You will need an overlap of about 75 mm (3 in) on all sides of the canvas so that you can fold it round the stretcher. Cut your piece of canvas accordingly. If you are stretching a piece of modern needlework you will need to measure this first and then buy the correct size of stretcher. Those of you who want to stretch a piece of tapestry or needlepoint which you have made from a piece of canvas with the design printed on it for you to follow should find that the manufacturers have left you just enough white border to fold around a stretcher. Measure the picture area and when you buy your stretcher, make sure that its outside edges fit exactly on this area.

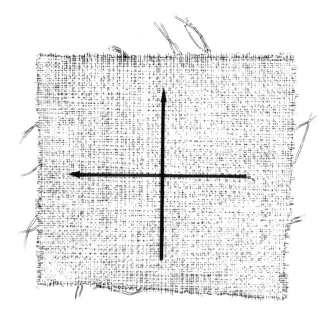

Fig. 57 The two arrows at right angles to each other indicate the warp and weft threads

If you are lucky enough to have found an old sample or some antique lace that you want to frame – or indeed, any piece of fragile cloth – you should sew very carefully along all its edges to a larger piece of stronger backing fabric and then stretch that round the stretcher. If you try to stretch anything that is weak or old it will tear. This subject is covered in greater depth in the chapter on framing a piece of needlework (see page 58).

All fabric is made up of threads called the warp and the weft, which run at right angles to each other. Do no

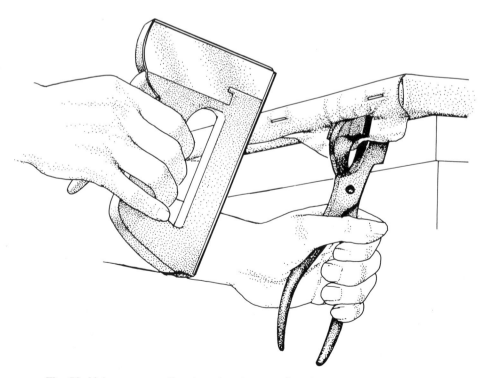

Fig. 58 Using canvas pliers to get a strong pull and even tension on the canvas

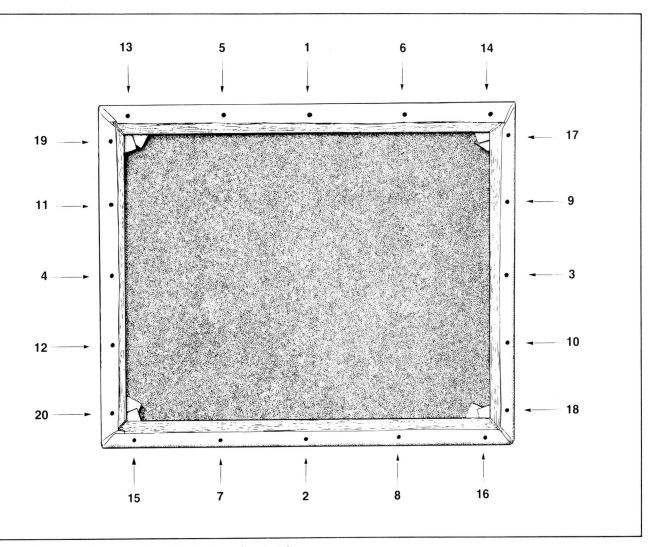

Fig. 59 Order of pinning or stapling the canvas to the stretcher

worry about which one is which; sometimes it is very difficult to tell. When the fabric is woven, the warp threads are the ones which run the length of the machine and the wefts run from side to side across the width of the cloth. All you need to remember is that they sit at right angles to each other. Now look at the back of your canvas and find the warp and weft threads (fig. 57). Using a soft pencil and a ruler, draw a faint line along them in both directions so that you have a cross in the middle of the canvas. Smooth the canvas out on your work surface and lay your stretcher on top. Centre the stretcher so that you can see the cross on the canvas clearly. The whole idea of stretching a canvas is to pin it under tension to the stretcher. This tension must be even over the whole of the fabric otherwise it will eventually sag and deform, and that can damage your painting. If, while you are pinning, you see that the cross on the back of the canvas is beginning to distort it means that you have applied the tension unevenly.

If you know you will be stretching your own canvas, and especially if you are stretching ready-primed canvas, you should invest in a pair of canvas pliers. This is really the only way to get a good pull on the canvas without taking the skin off your knuckles.

You should start by pulling the top edge of the canvas over the middle of the top of the stretcher and pinning it to the back, using either a large-headed tack or a staple gun (fig. 58). Then pull the canvas over the middle of the bottom edge of the stretcher and pin it in place. Do the same with the sides so that the canvas is attached to the middle of the four sides of the stretcher. You should be able to see the tension in the fabric, and the two pencil lines on the back should still be at right angles. If they are not, release the canvas and start again. Once you are satisfied that the canvas is evenly stretched, continue pinning it to the stretcher all the way round. Work from the middle of the stretcher to the corners, stretching the canvas from alternate sides (fig. 59). At the corners, make a neat tuck in the canvas and pin it down. If you are using unprimed canvas, give the back of it a light spray with clean water at this point and leave it to dry. Unprimed canvas shrinks slightly as

51

it dries and damping the canvas once it is stretched means that it dries under slight tension, producing a much firmer surface for you to paint on.

Most stretchers are sold with wedge-shaped pieces of wood called keys, which can be tapped into slots in the corners, thereby extending the size of the stretcher and thus ensuring that the canvas is absolutely taut. Many myths seem to have grown up about the use of these keys. In fact, they should only be used to correct the tension of the canvas while you are painting and for nothing else. Differences in humidity and temperature can cause the canvas to relax or tighten up slightly and it can be disturbing if the canvas feels as if it is under a totally different tension from one day to the next while you are trying to work. When you have finished painting you should tape the keys in place with brown paper tape so that they hold the corners of the stretcher firmly. The tape also stops them working loose over a matter of time and either getting lost or, even worse, falling down between the canvas and the stretcher so that they cause bumps on the front of the painting.

An old sagging canvas should be restretched by an expert. If your newly stretched canvas or needlework is loose or unevenly tensioned then you must take out the pins and start again. Tensioning the canvas by banging in the keys further will merely open up the corner of the stretcher, seriously weakening it as a structure. It is also likely to damage the corners of your picture.

Assembling the frame

Because you do not need a window mount if you are framing a work on a stretcher the measurements you need for the inside of the frame are the same as the outside edges of the stretcher. Measure the height and then the width of the stretched painting, then write the measurements down. These will correspond with the inside rebate measurements of the frame (**fig. 60**). Check with **fig. 6** if you cannot remember which part of the moulding is the inside rebate.

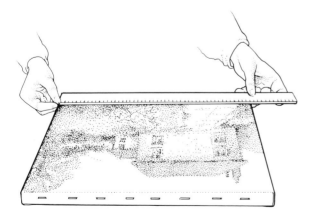

Fig. 60 Measuring the outside edge of the stretcher

Because I am trained as a conservator it is secon nature to me to try to treat any painting, or any part of painting, with great care. Conservators will always t to make a frame that will protect the work of art and n damage it in any way. There are two main areas where frame can damage a stretched painting. One is the side where the canvas is pulled round the stretcher, becaus over many years the fabric can become worn an fragile. In addition, the wooden stretcher will expan and contract, depending on the amount of moisture i the atmosphere; if the frame is tight up against th sides of the painting this movement can cause it t warp. The other area of potential damage is on the fron of the picture where it rests against the front rebate.

To avoid the first of these problems it is importar to leave a breathing space between the moulding an the sides of the painting, so add 4 mm (⅛ in) to each o your stretcher measurements. Let us suppose that th outside edges of your stretcher measure 300 × 200 mr (12 × 8 in). The inside rebate measurements of you frame should therefore be 304 × 204 mm (12⅛ × 8⅛ in Do not worry that the picture is going to rattle aroun in the frame; there are ways of coping with this, a you will see.

Making the frame   The frame for a painting on a car vas is made in exactly the same way as the watercolou frame described on page 16. Remember, howeve when you mark up your moulding ready to cut, that th measurements you have written down are the *insi* measurements of your frame. Proceed as explaine earlier with the cutting, glueing and pinning of you moulding. Make a pencil mark on the inside edge of th back rebate, put the moulding into the mitre box an line up the saw with your mark. Cut the mitred pieces c moulding as before and make up your frame. If yo intend to varnish, paint or stain the frame, do th before you go any further.

You should now try the frame for size against th painting. The picture should drop easily into the fram and rest against the front rebate, or against the glass i you are using it. If you have decided to glaze your fram you should seal in the glass with brown gum tape a described on page 23.

Fitting the frame   The next stage is to pack the frame s that the picture is held steady. At this point some com mercial framers might just give the keys at the back o the stretcher a good tap to knock it out so that the paint ing is pushed up tight against the frame. If you hav been reading carefully so far you will realize that this i a sure way to open the corners of the stretcher and dam age the canvas; jam the stretcher up against the sides o the frame so that over the years it rubs the canvas an weakens it; and allow the stretcher absolutely no roon to expand and contract naturally with changes ir

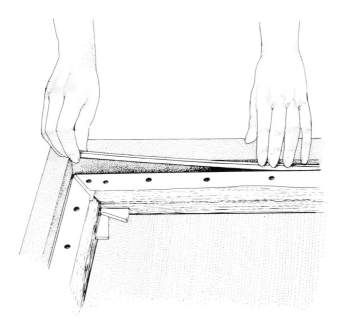

Fig. 61 Cutting Conservation Board strips and slipping them down between the stretcher and the frame

umidity, so that it eventually warps. And I am not too sure how you would get the painting out of the frame should you decide to have it cleaned, mended or reframed in the years to come. Presumably you would have to remove the keys, losing all of the tension on the picture and probably damaging the paint layer in the process, then restretch the painting afterwards.

A correct way to hold the picture steady within its frame is by means of strips of Conservation Board slipped gently down between the sides of the picture and the moulding (**fig. 61**). Because Conservation Board is quite soft it will cushion any expansion and contraction of the stretcher, and at the same time the board's smooth surface will protect the edges of the canvas. When you want to remove the picture from the frame, ease these strips out first and lift the painting out by the stretcher, making sure that your fingers do not touch the back of the canvas.

Now that you have sorted that out, remove everything from the frame for the time being so that you can deal with the front rebate. If you have glazed your frame you should cut Conservation Board slips the same width as the front rebate of the frame and fix them in place behind the glass with brown gum tape. This is done in the same way as the inside rebate of a watercolour frame is lined to stop the work touching the glazing in the cases when a front window mount is not used. It is most important that an oil or acrylic painting does not rest against the glazing. In fact, if you have used very thick paint in your pictures you should be careful that none of the impasto touches it either. If

necessary, cut two thicknesses of board for the slips or pin thin strips of balsa wood behind the glass to hold the picture well away from it (**fig. 62**). Balsa wood is a very light, soft wood, which can be cut with a knife. You can buy it in long thin strips from model shops.

Some of the really serious damage to unglazed oil or acrylic paintings is caused by the wooden rebate at the front of the frame. Over the years it can flatten the paint round the edges of the picture and in some cases even rub it away. One of the simplest and most elegant

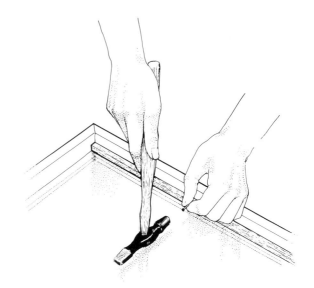

Fig. 62 Pinning balsa wood slips into the frame to hold the picture away from the glass

solutions to this problem is to line the front rebate with black velvet ribbon. You can buy this in various widths in most haberdashers and department stores. Choose a thin ribbon which will be hidden by the front rebate of the frame. Use only black ribbon since that blends in with the edge of the frame and does not show as a coloured line round the picture. Cut the ribbon to size and stick it behind the rebate using a good-quality wood-working adhesive (**fig. 63**). This ribbon should be sufficient to cushion the picture and protect the paint. If you are using balsa wood strips you should line them with ribbon in the same way.

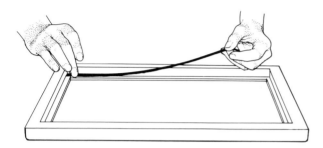

Fig. 63 Lining the front rebate of the frame with black velvet ribbon to cushion the picture

Next, put the frame face down on your work table and if you are using glass, give this a good clean. Then put your stretched picture carefully into the frame. Ease the Conservation Board slips into place round the edges of the stretcher. Check at the front to see that there are no bits of dust or dirt trapped in the frame.

Fitting the backboard You must now cut your backboard, which should be just large enough to drop neatly into the back of the frame. Secure it into the frame, using panel pins or the framer's gun I described in the chapter on backboards (see page 27). To make a really neat, professional job, seal round the edges of the backboard with brown gum tape.

You may be wondering why you should use a backboard in this kind of framing if you have not used glass on the front. Well, if you remember, creating a mini-atmosphere within the frame is only one of the reasons for using a strong backboard. Another important one is that it provides protection against knocks. As it stands, your canvas is rather like a stretched drumskin. However, unlike a drumskin, which is made from parchment and well able to withstand hard knocks, your canvas can be damaged by the slightest pressure; even the pressure of your fingers will cause dents if you pick it up too roughly. Not only will these dents and bumps show on the front, they will eventually cause the paint layer to crack. This, by the way, is the main reason why you should be very careful not to touch the back of

your painting when you lift it out of the frame by th stretcher.

There are many varied and no doubt apocrypha stories of accidents happening to paintings – one eve involving a fork-lift truck – where a strong backboar has saved the picture from certain destruction. Ther are equally some rather sad stories of cases where dam age to a picture could quite easily have been prevente by giving the frame a strong backboard.

When you get to the point of measuring and cuttin the backboard you might find you do not have room fo it inside the frame. After all, a stretcher takes up a lot o space. In this case, cut your backboard fractionall smaller than the outside edge measurements of th frame so that you can screw the backboard to the bac of the moulding. Once you have placed the backboar over the back of the frame you will need some way o knowing where the edges of the moulding are so tha you will not put a screw through the back of your pain ing by mistake. To indicate this, measure the width o the back edge of your moulding and draw a margin o the same width round the edges of your backboard. Us a bradawl or small drill bit to start the screw holes in th backboard and either countersink the holes or us screw cups. I always use brass screws and cups sinc they look professional and do not rust (**fig. 64**). Do nc screw the backboard to the stretcher as this would con strain the stretcher and it would probably warp eventu ally. That aside, remember that it is essential to attacl the backboard to the moulding in order to make th strong, six-sided, protective box needed for conserva tion framing.

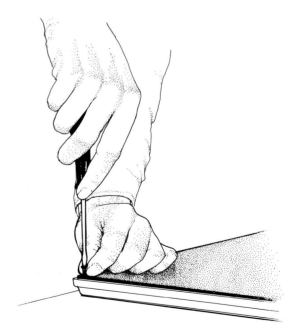

Fig. 64 Using brass screws and screw cups to screw the backboard onto the back edge of the moulding

You will probably find that, while there is not quite enough room inside the frame to take the backboard, there is nevertheless still a small space between the back of the stretcher and the backboard if you screw it on to the frame. This can also happen when you frame a work of art on paper. For example, you might have a print or drawing requiring a deep breathing space at the front of the frame to prevent it touching the glazing, which then doesn't leave quite enough room for the backboard to fit into the frame. To prevent a painting on a stretcher moving about inside the frame you can either pin it in place inside using panel pins or a framer's gun and then screw the backboard over the back of the frame; or you can pack the frame out to fill this gap and rest the backboard against the packing. Be very careful if you decide to pin the stretcher in place that you do not damage the back of it. If you are framing a work of art in a mount then you should always pack the back of the frame, if necessary, rather than use pins to hold it in place.

Always use acid-free Conservation Board to pack out a frame. Please do not use newspaper; it is very acidic and deteriorates quite quickly. You only have to leave some in bright sunlight for a few days to see it turn brown and brittle. New canvas is naturally slightly acidic and newspaper will cause it to deteriorate. Works of art on paper, of course, should never be left in acidic conditions.

Fig. 65 An unusual collection of paintings from the 1930s and 1940s. Some are in their original frames, while others need a moulding which is sympathetic to their period

55

THE LOWRY

And now a slight diversion! We have covered the conservation framing of a work of art on paper and also one that is stretched. I thought at this point you might be interested to learn how a museum approaches the framing of a valuable oil painting. The three major considerations for a museum are display; security from theft or tampering; and the protection of the painting, whether it is hanging in the gallery, cased in the hold of a jumbo jet on its way to an international exhibition, or just being held in storage. This chapter shows you how to frame your Rembrandts; or rather, in this case, a Lowry (**fig. 66**).

The back of the painting in its frame is illustrated in **fig. 67**. You should be able to see the edges of the stretcher and the back of the moulding. Take a good look at the canvas. It has been expertly stretched and the warp and weft threads are perfectly tensioned at

right angles to each other. The keys have been gent tapped in place and then taped so that they do not wo loose over time and fall down behind the stretcher ba If you look very closely between the edge of th stretcher and the frame you can just see the dark lin that is the black velvet ribbon which cushions the fro of the canvas. In fact, there is quite a large gap betwee the painting and the frame so the work is held in pla by eight small projections specially carved from co and taped in place with brown gum tape. Cork is dense but soft material. It gives support to the pictu and at the same time can absorb any jolts or knock without damaging the stretcher. The smooth surface the paper tape allows the painting to be slid out of th frame without damaging the fragile canvas on the side

The picture is secured in the frame not with pins b with brass mirror plates which have been bent so th

Fig. 66 *The Old House* by L. S. Lowry (*photo*: courtesy of the Tate Gallery)

Fig. 67 The back of the picture, fitted into the frame and ready for the backboard (*photo*: courtesy of the Tate Gallery)

hey rest gently on the back of the stretcher. In fact, the ends of the mirror plates have been fractionally curved upwards to prevent them rubbing against the canvas.

The back rebate on the original frame was very shallow; the decorative piece round the outer edge is part of t. In this case a lot of detailed construction work has aken place on the back of the original moulding in order to provide a deep enough rebate for the stretcher. Two hanging battens have been fixed to the top and bottom edges of the original frame. These are slightly deeper than the new rebate and are used to hang the picture securely on the wall with mirror plates.

The hardboard backboard is screwed into the back of the new rebate and sealed with brown gum tape **fig. 68**). The conservator has added a simple, neat piece of extra security: the edges of the backboard and he brown tape seal have several additional strips of ape across them which he has signed with a water-soluble ink. Anyone removing the backboard and tampering with the picture inside would automatically damage these seals.

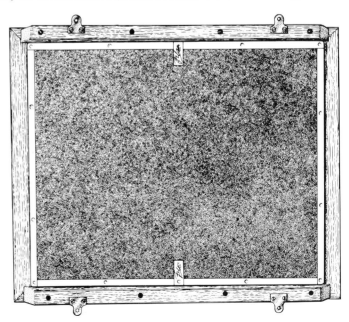

Fig. 68 The hardboard backboard has been screwed into place and sealed with brown paper

FRAMING NEEDLEWORK

Those of you who would like to frame a new piece of needlework which you have sewn from a kit or from your own design on to a heavy canvas fabric should refer back to the chapter on framing a work on a stretcher (see page 48), where I explain how to stretch your work round a wooden stretcher ready for framing.

In this chapter I want to elaborate slightly on how to prepare and mount an older, more fragile, or irregular piece of fabric. I have taken two examples: a fragment of an eighteenth-century Turkish carpet, measuring about 150 × 400 mm (6 × 16 in), which is illustrated in **fig. 69**; and an antique sampler (**fig. 70**). The methods described here should be used on anything that is old, fragile or valuable. Most things manage to be all three.

The carpet is robust enough to be sewn to a piece of backing fabric and stretched. I pinned the fragment out on to a larger piece of linen canvas and stitched it in place, using a fine needle and a coloured polyester thread which blended in with the backing fabric. This also gave me the opportunity to tack down any loose knots round the edges and straighten out the warps. When the fragment was sewn in place I stretched the canvas round the stretcher. In this way all of the tension was taken up by the canvas and not the carpet, which was far too fragile. The frame itself is a very deep one and the wooden slip, which holds the carpet away from the glass, has been lined with linen so that it matches the backing.

The sampler belongs to a friend. It was in an old frame, which she liked and wanted to retain, so the size of the backing board was limited by that. Normally I would suggest that you leave a greater margin between the work and the edge of the frame. Since you are by

now well into making your own frames this should be easy for you to do.

First I measured out the backing board so that it would fit the inside rebate of the frame. When you measure your own piece of needlework, add about 40 mm (1½ in) all round. You will need a reasonably thick backing board. Use a piece of Museum Board or stick together two thicknesses of Conservation Board and let them dry out thoroughly.

Next I had to cover my board with washed (and ironed) fine linen fabric. It was important to wash the fabric to remove any finishes or size that might have been used in its manufacture. I had no way of knowing what these might be and if they were likely to deteriorate over time. I cut my fabric about 75 mm (3 in) larger than the board all round, laid the board on top of it, and trimmed the corners. Then I pulled the fabric over the board and, using a good-quality wood-working adhesive, stuck it down on the back – first the top edge, then the bottom, then the sides – stretching it slightly as I pulled (**fig. 71**). When doing this it is important not to pull so hard that the board bows. This is why you need to use quite a thick board. I then made sure that the fabric weave was not distorted on the front and left it to dry under a weight.

Next day I carefully pinned the sampler out on to the linen-covered board and sewed it in place, using a curved needle and fine polyester thread (**fig. 72**). I also sewed carefully round the holes and damaged areas of the sampler, attaching them to the backing by means of tiny stitches and making sure I caused no more holes in the process.

The sampler and its backing were then reframed in the original frame, using balsa wood slips behind the glass to keep the needlework away from the glazing.

When preparing pieces of needlework such as these, choose a backing fabric that is sympathetic to the work and only slightly stronger than it. I used canvas behind the carpet, for example, because it is a robust piece of work in itself. The sampler could cope with a fine linen. A piece of lace might need a fine, good-quality cotton. Remember that all materials expand and contract over time. If you sew something very fragile on to a much stronger, robust fabric, the tensions you set up could eventually cause the backing to damage the original piece of work.

You should also try to use neutral-coloured fabrics wherever possible. Like the frame, the backing should display the work, not compete with it. However, if you

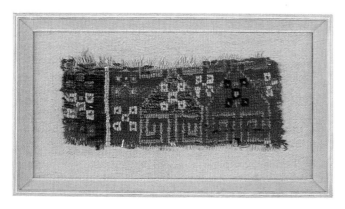

Fig. 69 A framed fragment of an eighteenth-century Turkish carpet

Fig. 70 A framed antique sampler and a selection of needlework

o choose a deeply coloured backing fabric, check first o see if the colour will run, or rub off, on to your needlework.

Some textile conservators use an adhesive to stick the original needlework to the backing fabric. This is a highly specialized process and they are trained to choose their adhesives and backings with great care. Most of the materials they use are not generally available. The methods I have given here might take longer but they have been chosen so that you could remove your needlework from its backing with the minimum of damage should the need arise.

Fig. 71 Attaching the linen to an acid-free board

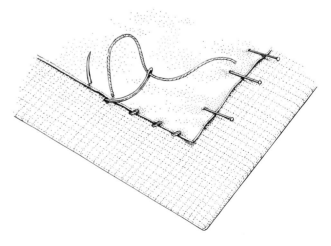

Fig. 72 Sewing the sampler onto the linen

TRANSPORTING PAINTINGS

Only by a slight stretch of the imagination, perhaps, could this chapter come under conservation framing, but I think it is important to include it under the general heading of protection. It is not unusual for a dealer or collector to buy a framed painting at the auction house, stick it in the back of his car and race straight round to his restorer. In the same way an artist will load up his car or van and set off for the gallery. Unfortunately, a surprising amount of damage can be done to the paintings on the way.

Single framed paintings can be carried safely in Daler-Rowney studio cases (**fig. 73**). These rigid plastic cases are made of polycarbonate, which is light but very strong, and waterproof. I also use them for carrying unframed works of art. Unmounted watercolours or drawings should be interleaved with Conservation Board or acid-free tissue paper to prevent them rubbing together and damaging the paint layer.

When dealing with several framed paintings th most vulnerable areas are the corners. To protect then pad them out with plastic foam, or even a good thic wad of newspaper (**fig. 74**). This will also stop ther leaning flat against each other. If the frames are le touching each other when they are being transported, sudden jolt could mean that the back of one fram smashes into the glazing of another.

Large, heavy frames should be interleaved wit sheets of expanded polystyrene. If you tape this i place, make sure that the tape does not touch the dec rated part of the moulding as it will damage paint su faces and gilding. If the pictures which are bein moved are glazed with glass, most galleries will stic masking tape over the surface. In the event that th glass does get broken, the tape will hold the broke pieces away from the picture. Again, if you do this, mak sure the tape does not touch the front of the moulding

Fig. 73 Daler-Rowney studio cases (*photo*: courtesy of Daler-Rowney)

Fig. 74 Protecting the corners of the frame

To be extra careful, wrap the whole painting and its wrapping in polythene or plastic sheeting. It may not be raining when you set off but the chances are it will be when you arrive!

Small paintings can be packed together in boxes. Wine buffs can use old wooden wine crates for this. If you use cardboard boxes then use several small ones rather than one large one, and tape all over the bottom of the box and up the sides with masking tape or a strong self-adhesive tape: cardboard boxes have a habit of collapsing just at the wrong moment, especially if they get wet.

If you need to transport a number of large paintings it would be better to hire a van so that they can be carried upright. Stack them against the sides of the van, interspersed with foam or some other soft material to prevent the frames touching each other. You will also need to put some wooden battening or thick foam on the floor of the van so that the bottom edges of the frames are cushioned. Then, using a stout rope or, even better, upholstery webbing, tie the pictures to the sides of the van. This is to keep them in place during the journey. The sound of a pile of pictures shifting from one side of the van to the other as you take a sharp left-hand bend is not easily forgotten.

The safe transportation of works of art is a subject that occupies most museums and galleries. There are, of course, specialist art transport firms which will deliver your paintings all over the world. On a less grand scale, if you want to do a more professional job yourself, it is possible to buy or hire well-designed packing cases (**fig. 75**). These are produced in a series of standard sizes, with packing materials to ensure that your picture fits snugly inside each case. The smaller cases can be taken as hand luggage on board planes.

Fig. 75 Art Network travelling cases (*photo*: courtesy of Tina Sitwell)

EXHIBITION AND STORAGE

If you have followed the instructions for conservation framing in this book you will have managed to give your works of art a good chance of surviving safely for many years. Yet even conservation framing cannot protect them from the damp basement or the leaking, sun-baked attic environment which seems to be the fate of many pictures. Try to store your paintings in a room which has moderate, stable conditions. This also applies to the rooms where you hang and exhibit them.

Some of the greatest and irredeemable damage is done to pictures by light. A bright light can fade some pigments so that they completely disappear and change others so that they are unrecognizable. The colours will fade at different rates, too. A watercolour of a sunset, for instance, can slowly change into an early morning scene as the red paint fades and the other pigments remain the same. Once this has happened to a work of art there is no way it can be restored.

Most of the immediate damage is caused by ultra-violet light in particular and fortunately this can be removed by special filters, either in the glazing or over the lights. But even these will not protect paintings from the damage caused by over-bright lighting. The amount of illumination given by direct sunlight, for instance, is too strong for most watercolours and will even cause the paper to change colour. Bright light will also cause most varnishes to yellow and will bleach the oil in oil paints.

It is very fashionable for modern galleries to illuminate their paintings with spotlights. However these are usually placed too close and can cause damage in two ways. First, the light is far too bright and shines on only part of the work, so that it not only fades

Fig. 76 (*above*) Spotlight with dichroic filter

Fig. 77 (*right*) Exhibiting pictures at home in subdued lighting and a stable atmosphere

he paint, it does so in patches; and second, if it is a tungsten lamp it heats up the picture, cooking a small area of it, which in extreme cases can actually cause the paint to blister.

Whether you are displaying your paintings at home or in a gallery, part of the latter problem, caused by too much heat, can be alleviated by using quartz-halogen lamps which are fitted with a dichroic filter (**fig. 76**). You can see these in most shop window displays where the window dresser wants to illuminate the goods without heating them. They are small spotlights with a cone-shaped reflector behind the bulb. This reflector throws most of the heat out from the back of the lamp instead of directing it forwards on to the display. They do, however, give out a very powerful light so their distance from the painting to be illuminated should be measured in metres rather than centimetres.

Displaying pictures at home

When hanging pictures at home common sense rather than science is the rule. Display your works in diffused lighting rather than under spotlights. Do not cook them over radiators or freeze them on chilly outside walls. **Fig. 77** shows the living room in a Georgian house which has been used to display the owner's collection of eighteenth-century watercolours. The room is north-facing and so gets no direct bright sunlight.

Perhaps the most important point of all is to try not to forget your paintings once they are hung. Our pictures tend to grow old alongside us and it is difficult to notice any changes. Take them off the wall at least once a year and look carefully to see if they are dirty, spotted, cracking or fading. In this way you should discover any potential damage before it is too late.

ABOUT THE AUTHOR

Fig. 78 Sheila Fairbrass working in her conservation studio

Sheila Fairbrass was born in Staffordshire. At the age of eighteen she went to Goldsmiths' College in South London where she studied painting while training to be a teacher. After completing the course she taught for four years in a school in south-east London. However, deciding she wanted a quieter life she left teaching and enrolled on the Paper Conservation course at Camberwell School of Art and Crafts. On completion she was employed as a paper conservator in the Conservation Department of the Tate Gallery, where she worked for ten years.

At that time over 90 per cent of the works of art in the gallery had permanent frames for display and storage. Conservators were expected to take an active part in the conservation of old frames and the design of new ones for modern works of art. They were also expected to make recommendations for the safety of works of art during transit to and while on display at other galleries. Because of her experience in this field, in 1986 Sheila Fairbrass was invited to speak at the Institute of Paper Conservation's Conference in Oxford on the problems of framing, exhibiting and storing large works of art on paper. This lecture has since been published in the Institute's journal.

In the same year she left the Tate Gallery and set up her own business as a freelance paper conservator in south-west London. Because of her continuing interest in education she takes every opportunity to teach and write. As part of the launch of *Framing* magazine, Sheila Fairbrass was asked to write a series of articles on paper conservation. She has also taken part in, and thoroughly enjoyed, the Magnolia Mouldings' Education Framing weekends, where she lectured on conservation for framers. In addition, she has organized for the staff of the British Council a series of seminars on the handling and display of works of art. She is occasionally invited back to the Paper Conservation course at Camberwell School of Art and Crafts to teach the students.

Sheila Fairbrass is a member of the publication committee for the United Kingdom Institute of Conservation and is the production editor for their annual journal. She was a founder member of the Institute of Paper Conservation and served on the first committee. She is also a Fellow of the International Institute of Conservation and a Fellow of the Royal Society of Art. In her spare time she is studying for a chemistry degree with the Open University.